JUDITH BUTLER

Giving an Account of Oneself

Fordham University Press

New York, 2005

Library of Congress Cataloging-in-Publication Data

   Butler, Judith.
      Giving an account of oneself / Judith Butler.—1st ed.
         p.   cm.
      Includes bibliographical references and index.
      ISBN 0-8232-2503-8 (hardcover) — ISBN 0-8232-2504-6 (pbk.)
   1. Self (Philosophy)   2. Ethics.   3. Conduct of life.   I. Title.
   BD450.B895   2005
   170'.42—dc22   2005017141

Printed in the United States of America
07 06   5 4 3
First edition

CONTENTS

ACKNOWLEDGMENTS

The chapters of this book were originally given as the Spinoza Lectures for the Department of Philosophy at the University of Amsterdam in the spring of 2002. I am grateful to Hent de Vries for extending that generous invitation and for the opportunity to work through some of this material with the students in Amsterdam. This work began as the topic of a faculty seminar at Princeton University in the fall of 2001, when I was a fellow at the Humanities Council. I gained an enormous amount from my discussions with faculty and students there. Finally, the material was delivered in revised form as the Adorno Lectures for the Institut für Sozialforschung in Frankfurt in the fall of 2002. I thank Axel Honneth for the opportunity to revisit and engage Adorno's work in a new way. I am equally grateful for discussions there with numerous individuals who offered me an intense engagement with the questions I raise. This text appeared in an earlier and substantially abbreviated form in the Netherlands as *Giving an Account of Oneself: A Critique of Ethical Violence* with Van Gorcum Press (2003) and subsequently appeared, again in abbreviated form, in German as *Kritik der Ethischen Gewalt* with Suhrkamp Verlag in 2003, ably translated by Reiner Ansen. Parts of Chapter Two appeared as an article entitled "Giving an Account of Oneself" in *Diacritics* 31.4:22–40.

My gratitude extends to several people who worked through various ideas in this manuscript with me: Frances Bartkowski, Jay Bernstein, Wendy Brown, Michel Feher, Barbara Johnson, Debra Keates, Paola Marrati, Biddy Martin, Jeff Nunokawa, Denise Riley, Joan W. Scott, Annika Thiem, and Niza Yanay. I am also grateful to the students in my comparative literature seminar in the fall of 2003, who read with me most of the texts considered here, challenging my perspectives and prompting intense debate on many of the topics. I thank Jill Stauffer for showing me the importance of Levinas for ethical thinking, and Colleen Pearl, Amy Jamgochian, Stuart Murray, James Salazar, Amy Huber, and Annika Thiem for editorial assistance and suggestions at various stages. And last, I thank Helen Tartar, who is willing to wrestle with my sentences and to whom, it appears, this book returns. It is dedicated to my friend and interlocutor Barbara Johnson.

The following abbreviations have been used in the text.

DF   Emmanuel Levinas, *Difficult Freedom: Essays on Judaism*. Trans. Sean Hand. Baltimore: The Johns Hopkins University Press, 1990.

FS   Michel Foucault, *Fearless Speech*. Ed. Joseph Pearson. New York: Semiotext(e), 2001.

GM   Friedrich Nietzsche, *On the Genealogy of Morals*. Trans. Walter Kaufmann. New York: Random House, 1969.

H   Michel Foucault, "About the Beginning of the Hermeneutics of the Self," trans. Thomas Keenan and Mark Blasius. In Michel Foucault, *Religion and Culture*, ed. Jeremy Carrette (New York: Routledge, 1999), 158–81.

HDS   Michel Foucault, *L'Herméneutique du sujet: Cours au Collège de France. 1981–82* (Paris: Gallimard, 2001).

HM   Michel Foucault, "How Much Does It Cost for Reason to Tell the Truth?" In *Foucault Live*, ed. Sylvère Lotringer, trans. John Honston. New York: *Semiotext(e)*, 1989.

OB   Emmanuel Levinas, *Otherwise than Being, or beyond Essence*. Trans. Alphonso Lingis. The Hague: Martinus Nijhoff, 1981.

PMP   Theodor W. Adorno, *Problems of Moral Philosophy*. Trans. Rodney Livingstone. Stanford: Stanford University Press, 2001.

S   "Substitution," originally published in *La Revue Philosophique du Louvain* 66 (1968), 487–508, translated by Peter Atterton, Simon

Critchley, and Graham Noctor in *Emmanuel Levinas, Basic Philosophical Writings,* ed. Adriaan T. Peperzak, Simon Critchley, and Robert Bernasconi (Bloomington: Indiana University Press, 1996), 79–96.

SP   Michel Foucault, "Structuralisme et poststructuralisme," in Foucault, *Dits et Ecrits, 1954–1988,* vol. 4 (Paris: Gallimard), 431–457. Translations that refer directly to this text in French are my own.

UP   Michel Foucault, *The Use of Pleasure: The History of Sexuality, Volume Two.* New York: Random House, 1985.

In this book, I use the notion of the "other" to denote the human other in its specificity except where, for technical reasons, the term needs to mean something slightly different. In Levinas, for instance, "the Other" not only refers to the human other but acts as a place-holder for an infinite ethical relation. In the latter case, I've capitalized the term.

Giving an Account of Oneself

ONE

An Account of Oneself

The value of thought is measured by its distance from the continuity of the familiar.

—Adorno, *Minima Moralia*

I would like to begin by considering how it might be possible to pose the question of moral philosophy, a question that has to do with conduct and, hence, with doing, within a contemporary social frame. To pose this question in this way is already to admit to a prior thesis, namely, that moral questions not only emerge in the context of social relations, but that the form these questions take changes according to context, and even that context, in some sense, inheres in the form of the question. In *Problems of Moral Philosophy*, a set of lectures given in the summer of 1963, Adorno writes, "We can probably say that moral questions have always arisen when moral norms of behaviour have ceased to be self-evident and unquestioned in the life of a community."[1] In a way, this claim seems to give an account of the conditions under which moral questions arise, but Adorno further specifies the account. There he offers a brief critique of Max Scheler, who laments the *Zersetzung* of ethical ideas, by which he means the destruction of a common and collective ethical ethos.

Adorno refuses to mourn this loss, worrying that the collective ethos is invariably a conservative one, which postulates a false unity that attempts to suppress the difficulty and discontinuity existing within any contemporary ethos. It is not that there was once a unity that subsequently has come apart, only that there was once an idealization, indeed, a nationalism, that is no longer credible, and ought not to be. As a result, Adorno cautions against the recourse to ethics as a certain kind of repression and violence. He writes:

> nothing is more degenerate than the kind of ethics or morality that survives in the shape of collective ideas even after the World Spirit has ceased to inhabit them—to use the Hegelian expression as a kind of shorthand. Once the state of human consciousness and the state of social forces of production have abandoned these collective ideas, these ideas acquire repressive and violent qualities. And what forces philosophy into the kind of reflections that we are expressing here is the element of compulsion which is to be found in traditional customs; it is this violence and evil that brings these customs [*Sitten*] into conflict with morality [*Sittlichkeit*]—and not the decline of morals of the kind lamented by the theoreticians of decadence. (*PMP*, 17)

In the first instance, Adorno makes the claim that moral questions arise only when the collective ethos has ceased to hold sway. This implies that moral questions do not have to arise on the basis of a commonly accepted ethos to qualify as such; indeed, there seems to be a tension between ethos and morality, such that a waning of the former is the condition for the waxing of the latter. In the second instance, he makes clear that although the collective ethos is no longer shared—indeed, precisely because the collective ethos, which must now be herded by quotation marks, is not commonly shared—it can impose its claim to commonality only through violent means. In this sense, the collective ethos instrumentalizes violence to maintain the appearance of its collectivity. Moreover, this ethos becomes violence only once it has become an anachronism. What is strange historically—and temporally—about this form of ethical violence is that although the collective ethos has become anachronistic, it has not become past; it insists itself into the present as an anachronism. The ethos refuses to become past, and violence is the way in which it imposes itself upon the present. Indeed, it not only imposes itself upon the present, but also seeks to eclipse the present—and this is precisely one of its violent effects.

Adorno uses the term *violence* in relation to ethics in the context of claims about universality. He offers yet another formulation of the emergence of morality, which is always the emergence of certain kinds of moral inquiry, of moral questioning: "the social problem of the divergence between the universal interest and the particular interest, the interests of particular individuals, is what goes to make up the problem of morality" (*PMP*, 19). What are the conditions under which this divergence takes place? He refers to a situation in which "the universal" fails to agree with or include the individual and the claim of universality itself ignores the "rights" of the individual. We can imagine, for instance, the imposition of governments on foreign countries in the name of universal principles of democracy, where the imposition of the government effectively denies the rights of the population at issue to elect its own officials. We might, along these lines, think about President Bush's proposal for the Palestinian Authority or his efforts to replace the government in Iraq. In these instances, to use Adorno's words, "the universal . . . appears as something violent and extraneous and has no substantial reality for human beings" (*PMP*, 19). Although Adorno sometimes moves abruptly between ethics and morality, he prefers the term *morality*, echoed later in *Minima Moralia*, for his project and insists that any set of maxims or rules must be appropriable by individuals "in a living way" (*PMP*, 15). Whereas one might reserve *ethics* for the broad contours of these rules and maxims, or for the relation between selves that is implied by such rules, Adorno insists that an ethical norm that fails to offer a way to live or that turns out, within existing social conditions, to be impossible to appropriate has to become subject to critical revision (*PMP*, 19). If it ignores the existing social conditions, which are also the conditions under which any ethics might be appropriated, that ethos becomes violent.

In this first chapter of what follows, I want to indicate what I take to be important about Adorno's conception of ethical violence, although I will postpone a more systematic consideration until Chapter Three. In my introductory section, I want simply to point out the importance of his formulation for contemporary debates about moral nihilism and to show how changes in his theoretical framework are necessitated by the shifting historical character of moral inquiry itself. In a sense, this shift beyond Adorno is one he might have condoned, given his commitment to considering morality within the changing social contexts in which the need for moral inquiry emerges. The context is not exterior to the question; it conditions the form that the question will take. In this sense, the questions that characterize moral inquiry are formulated or stylized by the historical conditions that prompt them.

I take it that Adorno's critique of abstract universality as violent can be read in relation to Hegel's critique of the kind of abstract universality characteristic of The Terror. I have written about that elsewhere,[2] and wish only to remark here that the problem is not with universality as such but with an operation of universality that fails to be responsive to cultural particularity and fails to undergo a reformulation of itself in response to the social and cultural conditions it includes within its scope of applicability. When a universal precept cannot, for social reasons, be appropriated or when—indeed, for social reasons—it must be refused, the universal precept itself becomes a site of contest, a theme and an object of democratic debate. That is to say, it loses its status as a precondition of democratic debate; if it did operate there as a precondition, as a *sine qua non* of participation, it would impose its violence in the form of an exclusionary foreclosure. This does not mean that universality is by definition violent. It is not. But there are conditions under which it can exercise violence. Adorno helps us to understand that its violence consists in part in its indifference to the social conditions under which a living appropriation might become possible. If no living appropriation is possible, then it would seem to follow that the precept can be undergone only as a deathly thing, a suffering imposed from an indifferent outside at the expense of freedom and particularity.

Adorno seems nearly Kierkegaardian in insisting upon the place and meaning of the existing individual and the necessary task of appropriating morality as well as opposing forms of ethical violence. But of course he cautions against the error to be found in the opposite position, when the "I" becomes understood apart from its social conditions, when it is espoused as a pure immediacy, arbitrary or accidental, detached from its social and historical conditions—which, after all, constitute the general conditions of its own emergence. He is clear that there is no morality without an "I," but pressing questions remain: In what does that "I" consist? And in what terms can it appropriate morality or, indeed, give an account of itself? He writes, for instance, "it will be obvious to you that all ideas of morality or ethical behavior must relate to an 'I' that acts" (*PMP*, 28). Yet there is no "I" that can fully stand apart from the social conditions of its emergence, no "I" that is not implicated in a set of conditioning moral norms, which, being norms, have a social character that exceeds a purely personal or idiosyncratic meaning.

The "I" does not stand apart from the prevailing matrix of ethical norms and conflicting moral frameworks. In an important sense, this matrix is also the condition for the emergence of the "I," even though the "I" is not causally induced by those norms. We cannot conclude that the "I" is simply the effect or the instrument of some prior ethos or some field of conflicting or discontinuous norms. When the "I" seeks to give an account of itself, it can start with itself, but it will find that this self is already implicated in a social temporality that exceeds its own capacities for narration; indeed, when the "I" seeks to give an account of itself, an account that must include the conditions of its own emergence, it must, as a matter of necessity, become a social theorist.

The reason for this is that the "I" has no story of its own that is not also the story of a relation—or set of relations—to a set of norms. Although many contemporary critics worry that this means there is no concept of the subject that can serve as the ground for moral agency and moral accountability, that conclusion does not follow. The "I" is always to some extent dispossessed by the social conditions of its emergence.[3] This dispossession does not mean that we have lost the subjective ground for ethics. On the contrary, it may well be the condition for moral inquiry, the condition under which morality itself emerges. If the "I" is not at one with moral norms, this means only that the subject must deliberate upon these norms, and that part of deliberation will entail a critical understanding of their social genesis and meaning. In this sense, ethical deliberation is bound up with the operation of critique. And critique finds that it cannot go forward without a consideration of how the deliberating subject comes into being and how a deliberating subject might actually live or appropriate a set of norms. Not only does ethics find itself embroiled in the task of social theory, but social theory, if it is to yield nonviolent results, must find a living place for this "I."

There are a variety of ways to account for the emergence of the "I" from the matrix of social institutions, ways of contextualizing morality within its social conditions. Adorno tends to understand a negative dialectics to be at work when claims of collectivity turn out *not* to be collective, when claims of abstract universality turn out *not* to be universal. The divergence is always between the universal and the particular, and it becomes the condition for moral questioning. The universal not only diverges from the particular, but this very divergence is what the individual comes to experience, what becomes for the individual the inaugural experience of morality. In this sense, Adorno's theory resonates with Nietzsche, who underscores the violence of "bad conscience," which brings the "I" into being as a consequence of a potentially annihilating cruelty. The "I" turns against itself, unleashing its morally condemning aggression against itself, and thus reflexivity is inaugurated. At least this is the Nietzschean view of bad conscience. I would suggest that Adorno alludes to such a negative view of bad conscience when he maintains that an ethics that cannot be appropriated in "a living way" by individuals under socially existing conditions "is the bad conscience of conscience" (*PMP*, 15).

We must ask, however, whether the "I" who must appropriate moral norms in a living way is not itself conditioned by norms, norms that establish the viability of the subject. It is one thing to say that a subject must be able to appropriate norms, but another to say that there must be norms that prepare a place within the ontological field for a subject. In the first instance, norms are there, at an exterior distance, and the task is to find a way of appropriating them, taking them on, establishing a living relation to them. The epistemological frame is presupposed in this encounter, one in which a subject encounters moral norms and must find his way with them. But did Adorno consider that norms also decide in advance who will and will not become a subject? Did he consider the operation of norms in the very constitution of the subject, in the stylization of its ontology and in the establishing of a legitimate site within the realm of social ontology?

Scenes of Address

> We begin with a response, a question that answers to a noise, and we do it in the dark—doing without exactly knowing, making do with speaking. Who's there, or here, and who's gone?
>
> —Thomas Keenan, *Fables of Responsibility*

For the moment, I will take leave of this discussion of Adorno, though I will return to him later to consider, not the relation that a subject has to morality, but a prior relation: the force of morality in the production of the subject. The first question is a crucial one and is not obviated by the investigation that follows, because a subject produced by morality must find his or her relation to morality. One cannot will away this paradoxical condition for moral deliberation and for the task of giving an account of oneself. Even if morality supplies a set of norms that produce a subject in his or her intelligibility, it also remains a set of norms and rules that a subject must negotiate in a living and reflective way.

In *On the Genealogy of Morals*, Nietzsche offers a controversial account of how we become reflective at all about our actions and how we become positioned to give an account of what we have done. He remarks that we become conscious of ourselves only after certain injuries have been inflicted. Someone suffers as a consequence, and the suffering person or, rather, someone acting as his or her advocate in a system of justice seeks to find the cause of that suffering and asks us whether we might be that cause. It is in the interest of meting out a just punishment to the one responsible for an injurious action that the question is posed and that the subject in question comes to question him or herself. "Punishment," Nietzsche tells us, is "the making of a memory."[4] The question posits the self as a causative force, and it also models a specific mode of responsibility. In asking whether we caused such suffering, we are being asked by an established authority not only to avow a causal link between our own actions and the suffering that follows but also to take responsibility for these actions and their effects. In this context, we find ourselves in the position of having to give an account of ourselves.

We start to give an account only because we are interpellated as beings who are rendered accountable by a system of justice and punishment. This system is not there from the start, but becomes instituted over time and at great cost to the human instincts. Nietzsche writes that, under these conditions, people "felt unable to cope with the simplest undertakings; in this new world they no longer possessed their former guides, their regulating, unconscious, and infallible drives: they were reduced to thinking, inferring, reckoning, co-ordinating cause and effect, these unfortunate creatures; they were reduced to their 'consciousness,' their weakest and most fallible organ!" (*GM*, 84).

So I start to give an account, if Nietzsche is right, because someone has asked me to, and that someone has power delegated from an established system of justice. I have been addressed, even perhaps had an act attributed to me, and a certain threat of punishment backs up this interrogation. And so, in fearful response, I offer myself as an "I" and try to reconstruct my deeds, showing that the deed attributed to me was or was not, in fact, among them. I am either owning up to myself as the cause of such an action, qualifying my causative contribution, or defending myself against the attribution, perhaps locating the cause elsewhere. These are the parameters within which my account of myself takes place. For Nietzsche, accountability follows only upon an accusation or, minimally, an allegation, one made by someone in a position to deal out punishment if causality can be established. And we become reflective upon ourselves, accordingly, through fear and terror. Indeed, we become morally accountable as a consequence of fear and terror.

But let us consider that being addressed by another carries other valences besides fear. There may well be a desire to know and understand that is not fueled by the desire to punish, and a desire to explain and narrate that is not prompted by a terror of punishment. Nietzsche did well to understand that I begin my story of myself only in the face of a "you" who asks me to give an account. Only in the face of such a query or attribution from an other—"Was it you?"—do any of us start to narrate ourselves, or find that, for urgent reasons, we must become self-narrating beings. Of course, it is always possible to remain silent in the face of such a question, where the silence articulates a resistance to the question: "You have no right to ask such a question," or "I will not dignify this allegation with a response," or "Even if it was me, this is not for you to know." Silence in these instances either calls into question the legitimacy of the authority invoked by the question and the questioner or attempts to circumscribe a domain of autonomy that cannot or should not be intruded upon by the questioner. The refusal to narrate remains a relation to narrative and to the scene of address. As a narrative withheld, it either refuses the relation that the inquirer presupposes or changes that relation so that the one queried refuses the one who queries.

Telling a story about oneself is not the same as giving an account of oneself. And yet we can see in the example above that the kind of narrative required in an account we give of ourselves accepts the presumption that the self has a causal relation to the suffering of others (and eventually, through bad conscience, to oneself). Not all narrative takes this form, clearly, but a narrative that responds to allegation must, from the outset, accept the possibility that the self has causal agency, even if, in a given instance, the self may not have been the cause of the suffering in question.

Giving an account thus takes a narrative form, which not only depends upon the ability to relay a set of sequential events with plausible transitions but also draws upon narrative voice and authority, being directed toward an audience with the aim of persuasion. The narrative must then establish that the self either was or was not the cause of that suffering, and so supply a persuasive medium through which to understand the causal agency of the self. The narrative does not emerge after the fact of causal agency but constitutes the prerequisite condition for any account of moral agency we might give. In this sense, narrative capacity constitutes a precondition for giving an account of oneself and assuming responsibility for one's actions through that means. Of course, one might simply "nod" or make use of another expressive gesture to acknowledge that one is indeed the one who authored the deed in question. The "nod" functions as an expressive precondition of acknowledgment. A similar kind of expressive power is at work when one remains silent in the face of the query "Do you have anything to say for yourself?" In both examples, though, the gesture of acknowledgment makes sense only in relation to an implied story line: "Yes, I was the one who occupied the position of the causal agent in the sequence of events to which you refer."

Nietzsche's view does not fully take into account the scene of address through which responsibility is queried and then either accepted or denied. He assumes that the query is made from within a legal framework in which punishment is threatened as an equivalent injury for the injury committed in the first place. But not all forms of address originate from this system and for this reason. The system of punishment he describes is based on revenge, even when that is valorized as "justice." That system does not recognize that life entails a certain amount of suffering and injury that cannot be fully accounted for through recourse to the subject as a causal agent. Indeed, for Nietzsche aggression is coextensive with life, so that if we sought to outlaw aggression, we would effectively be trying to outlaw life itself. He writes that "life operates *essentially*, that is in its basic functions, through injury, assault, exploitation, destruction and cannot be thought of at all without this character" (*GM*, 76). "Legal conditions," he writes further on, "constitute a partial restriction on the will of life," a will that is defined by struggle. The legal effort to obliterate struggle would be, in his words, "an attempt to assassinate the future of man" (ibid.).

At stake for Nietzsche is not simply the prevalence of a morality and legal order he opposes but a coerced crafting of the "human" in opposition to life itself. His view of life, however, assumes that aggression is more primary than generosity and that concerns for justice emerge from a revenge ethic. He fails to consider the interlocutory scene in which one is asked what one has done, or a situation in which one tries to make plain, to one who is waiting to know, what one has done, and for what reason.

For Nietzsche, the self as "cause" of an injurious action is always retroactively attributed—the doer is only belatedly attached to the deed. In fact, the doer becomes the causal agent of the deed only through a retroactive attribution that seeks to comply with a moral ontology stipulated by a legal system, one that establishes accountability and punishable offenses by locating a relevant self as a causal source of suffering. For Nietzsche, suffering exceeds any effect caused by one self or another, and though there are clearly instances when one vents aggression externally against another, causing injury or destruction, there is something "justifiable" about this suffering to the extent that it is part of life and constitutes part of the "seduction" and "vitality" of life itself. There are many reasons to quarrel with this account, and I'll make some of my own differences clear as I proceed.

Importantly, Nietzsche restricts his understanding of accountability to this juridically mediated and belated attribution. Apparently he fails to understand the other interlocutory conditions in which one is asked to give an account of oneself, focusing instead on an original aggression that he holds to be part of every human being and, indeed, coextensive with life itself. Its prosecution under a system of punishment would, in his view, eradicate this truth about life. The institution of law compels an originally aggressive human to turn that aggression "inward," to craft an inner world composed of a guilty conscience and to vent that aggression against oneself in the name of morality: "in this psychical cruelty there resides a madness of the will which is absolutely unexampled; the *will* of man to find himself guilty and reprehensible to a degree that can never be atoned for" (*GM*, 93). This aggression, which Nietzsche regards as native to every human animal and to life itself, is turned against the will and then assumes a second life, imploding to construct a conscience that generates reflexivity on the model of self-beratement. That reflexivity is the precipitate of the subject, understood as a reflexive being, one who can and does take him or herself as an object of reflection.

As I mentioned above, Nietzsche does not consider other linguistic dimensions of this situation. If I am held accountable through a framework of morality, that framework is first addressed to me, first starts to act upon me, through the address and query of another. Indeed, I come to know that framework through no other way. If I give an account of myself in response to such a query, I am implicated in a relation to the other before whom and to whom I speak. Thus, I come into being as a reflexive subject in the context of establishing a narrative account of myself when I am spoken to by someone and prompted to address myself to the one who addresses me.

In *The Psychic Life of Power*,[5] I perhaps too quickly accepted this punitive scene of inauguration for the subject. According to that view, the institution of punishment ties me to my deed, and when I am punished for having done this or that deed, I emerge as a subject of conscience and, hence, a subject who reflects upon herself in some way. This view of subject formation depends upon an account of a subject who internalizes the law or, minimally, the causal tethering of the subject to the deed for which the institution of punishment seeks compensation.

One might expect this Nietzschean account of punishment to become crucial to Foucault's account of disciplinary power in the prison. It surely was, but Foucault differs explicitly from Nietzsche by refusing to generalize the scene of punishment to account for how a reflexive subject comes about. The turning against oneself that typifies the emergence of Nietzschean bad conscience does not account for the emergence of reflexivity in Foucault. In *The Use of Pleasure*, the second volume of *The History of Sexuality*,[6] Foucault examines the conditions under which a self might take itself to be an object for reflection and cultivation, concentrating on premodern formations of the subject. Whereas Nietzsche thinks ethics can be derived from a terrorizing scene of punishment, Foucault, departing from the final reflections in *On the Genealogy of Morals*, focuses on the peculiar creativity in which morality engages and how it is, in particular, that bad conscience becomes the means for manufacturing values. For Nietzsche, morality emerges as the terrorized response to punishment. But this terror turns out to be strangely fecund; morality and its precepts (soul, conscience, bad conscience, consciousness, self-reflection, and instrumental reasoning) are all soaked in cruelty and aggression turned back upon itself. The elaboration of a morality—a set of rules and equivalences—is the sublimated (and inverted) effect of this primary aggression turned against oneself, the idealized consequence of a turn against one's own destructiveness and, for Nietzsche, one's own life impulses.

Indeed, whereas Nietzsche considers the force of punishment to be instrumental to the internalization of rage and the consequent production of bad conscience (and other moral precepts), Foucault turns increasingly to codes of morality, understood as codes of conduct—and *not* primarily to codes of punishment—to consider how subjects are constituted in relation to such codes, which do not always rely on the violence of prohibition and its internalizing effects. Nietzsche's masterly account in *On the Genealogy of Morals* shows us how, for instance, rage and spontaneous will are internalized to produce the sphere of the "soul" as well as a sphere of morality. This process of internalization is to be understood as an inversion, a turning of primarily aggressive impulse back on itself, the signature action of bad conscience. For Foucault, reflexivity emerges in the act of taking up a relation to moral codes, but it does not rely on an account of internalization or of psychic life more generally, certainly not a reduction of morality to bad conscience.

If one reads Nietzsche's critique of morality alongside Freud's assessment of conscience in *Civilization and Its Discontents* or his account of the aggressive basis of morality in *Totem and Taboo*, one might arrive at a fully cynical view of morality and conclude that human conduct that seeks to follow norms of prescriptive value is motivated less by any desire to do good than by a terrorized fear of punishment and its injurious effects. I'll save that comparative reading for another occasion. Here it seems important to note how much Foucault wanted to move away from this particular model and conclusion when, in the early 1980s, he decided to rethink the sphere of ethics. His interest shifted to a consideration of how certain historically established prescriptive codes compelled a certain kind of subject formation. Whereas in his earlier work, he treats the subject as an "effect" of discourse, in his later writings he nuances and refines his position as follows: The subject forms itself in relation to a set of codes, prescriptions, or norms and does so in ways that not only (a) reveal self-constitution to be a kind of *poiesis* but (b) establish self-making as part of the broader operation of critique. As I've argued elsewhere,[7] ethical self-making in Foucault is not a radical creation of the self *ex nihilo* but what he terms a "delimit[ing] of that part of the self that will form the object of his moral practice" (*UP*, 28). This work on the self, this act of delimiting, takes place within the context of a set of norms that precede and exceed the subject. These are invested with power and recalcitrance, setting the limits to what will be considered to be an intelligible formation of the subject within a given historical scheme of things. There is no making of oneself (*poiesis*) outside of a mode of subjectivation (*assujettisement*) and, hence, no self-making outside of the norms that orchestrate the possible forms that a subject may take. The practice of critique then exposes the limits of the historical scheme of things, the epistemological and ontological horizon within which subjects come to be at all. To make oneself in such a way that one exposes those limits is precisely to engage in an aesthetics of the self that maintains a critical relation to existing norms. In the 1978 lecture "What Is Critique?" Foucault writes: "Critique would insure the desubjugation of the subject in the course of what we could call, in a word, the politics of truth."[8]

In the introduction to *The Use of Pleasure*, Foucault specifies this practice of self-stylization in relation to norms when he makes clear that moral conduct is a question neither of conforming to the prescriptions entailed by a given code nor of internalizing a primary prohibition or interdiction. He writes:

> for an action to be "moral," it must not be reducible to an act or a series of acts conforming to a rule, a law, or a value. Of course all moral action involves a relationship with the reality in which it is carried out, and a relationship with the self. The latter is not simply "self-awareness" but self-formation as an "ethical subject," a process in which the individual delimits that part of himself that will form the object of his moral practice, defines his position relative to the precept he will follow, and decides on a certain mode of being that will serve as his moral goal. And this requires him to act upon himself, to monitor, test, improve, and transform himself. There is no specific moral action that does not refer to a unified moral conduct; no moral conduct that does not call for the forming of oneself as an ethical subject; and no forming of the ethical subject without "modes of subjectivation" and an "ascetics" or "practices of the self" that support them. Moral action is indissociable from these forms of self-activity. (*UP*, 28)

For Foucault, as for Nietzsche, morality redeploys a creative impulse. Nietzsche laments that the internalization of morality takes place through debilitation of the will, even though he understands that this internalization constitutes "the womb of all ideal and imaginative phenomena" (*GM*, 87), which would include, presumably, his own philosophical writing, together with this very account.

For Foucault, morality is inventive, requires inventiveness, and even, as we shall consider later, comes at a certain price. However, the "I" engendered by morality is not conceived as a self-berating psychic agency. From the outset, what relation the self will take to itself, how it will craft itself in response to an injunction, how it will form itself, and what labor it will perform upon itself is a challenge, if not an open question. The injunction compels the act of self-making or self-crafting, which means that it does not act unilaterally or deterministically upon the subject. It sets the stage for the subject's self-crafting, which always takes place in relation to an imposed set of norms. The norm does not produce the subject as its necessary effect, nor is the subject fully free to disregard the norm that inaugurates its reflexivity; one invariably struggles with conditions of one's own life that one could not have chosen. If there is an operation of agency or, indeed, freedom in this struggle, it takes place in the context of an enabling and limiting field of constraint. This ethical agency is neither fully determined nor radically free. Its struggle or primary dilemma is to be produced by a world, even as one must produce oneself in some way. This struggle with the unchosen conditions of one's life, a struggle—an agency—is also made possible, paradoxically, by the persistence of this primary condition of unfreedom.

Whereas many critics have claimed that the view of the subject proffered by Foucault—and other poststructuralists—undermines the capacity to conduct ethical deliberations and to ground human agency, Foucault turns both to agency and to deliberation in new ways in his so-called ethical writings and offers a reformulation of both that deserves a serious consideration. In the final chapter, I'll analyze more closely his attempt to provide an account of himself. Here I would like to turn to the more general question: Does the postulation of a subject who is not self-grounding, that is, whose conditions of emergence can never fully be accounted for, undermine the possibility of responsibility and, in particular, of giving an account of oneself?

If it is really true that we are, as it were, divided, ungrounded, or incoherent from the start, will it be impossible to ground a notion of personal or social responsibility? I will argue otherwise by showing how a theory of subject formation that acknowledges the limits of self-knowledge can serve a conception of ethics and, indeed, responsibility. If the subject is opaque to itself, not fully translucent and knowable to itself, it is not thereby licensed to do what it wants or to ignore its obligations to others. The contrary is surely true. The opacity of the subject may be a consequence of its being conceived as a relational being, one whose early and primary relations are not always available to conscious knowledge. Moments of unknowingness about oneself tend to emerge in the context of relations to others, suggesting that these relations call upon primary forms of relationality that are not always available to explicit and reflective thematization. If we are formed in the context of relations that become partially irrecoverable to us, then that opacity seems built into our formation and follows from our status as beings who are formed in relations of dependency.

This postulation of a primary opacity to the self that follows from formative relations has a specific implication for an ethical bearing toward the other. Indeed, if it is precisely by virtue of one's relations to others that one is opaque to oneself, and if those relations to others are the venue for one's ethical responsibility, then it may well follow that it is precisely by virtue of the subject's opacity to itself that it incurs and sustains some of its most important ethical bonds.

In the rest of this chapter, I will begin by examining Foucault's later theory of subject formation and will consider the limitations one encounters when one tries to use it to think the other. I will then proceed to a post-Hegelian account of recognition that seeks to establish the social basis for giving an account of oneself. In this context, I will consider the critique of a Hegelian model of recognition offered by Adriana Cavarero, a feminist philosopher who draws on the work of Levinas and Arendt.[9] In Chapter Two, I will turn to psychoanalysis and to the limits the unconscious imposes on the narrative reconstruction of a life. Although we are compelled to give an account of our various selves, the structural conditions of that account will turn out to make a full such giving impossible. The singular body to which a narrative refers cannot be captured by a full narration, not only because the body has a formative history that remains irrecoverable by reflection, but because primary relations are formative in ways that produce a necessary opacity in our understanding of ourselves. An account of oneself is always given to another, whether conjured or existing, and this other establishes the scene of address as a more primary ethical relation than a reflexive effort to give an account of oneself. Moreover, the very terms by which we give an account, by which we make ourselves intelligible to ourselves and to others, are not of our making. They are social in character, and they establish social norms, a domain of unfreedom and substitutability within which our "singular" stories are told.

I make eclectic use of various philosophers and critical theorists in this inquiry. Not all of their positions are compatible with one another, and I do not attempt to synthesize them here. Although synthesis is not my aim, I do want to maintain that each theory suggests something of ethical importance that follows from the limits that condition any effort one might make to give an account of oneself. Following from this, I want to argue that what we often consider to be ethical "failure" may well have an ethical valence and importance that has not been rightly adjudicated by those who too quickly equate poststructuralism with moral nihilism.

In Chapter Three, I consider diachronic and synchronic efforts to establish the emergence of the subject, including the ethical implications of these accounts of subject formation. I also study Adorno's contribution to a theory of responsibility that can negotiate between the so-called human and inhuman dimensions of ethical dispositions, examining how a critical politics is related to an ethics and, indeed, a morality that at times requires a first-person account of oneself. I hope to show that morality is neither a symptom of its social conditions nor a site of transcendence of them, but rather is essential to the determination of agency and the possibility of hope. With the help of Foucault's self-criticism, it may be possible to show that the question of ethics emerges precisely at the limits of our schemes of intelligibility, the site where we ask ourselves what it might mean to continue in a dialogue where no common ground can be assumed, where one is, at it were, at the limits of what one knows yet still under the demand to offer and receive acknowledgment: to someone else who is there to be addressed and whose address is there to be received.

Foucaultian Subjects

In Foucault's account of self-constitution, a question that emerges centrally in his work of the 1980s, a regime of truth offers the terms that make self-recognition possible. These terms are outside the subject to some degree, but they are also presented as the available norms through which self-recognition can take place, so that what I can "be," quite literally, is constrained in advance by a regime of truth that decides what will and will not be a recognizable form of being. Although the regime of truth decides in advance what form recognition can take, it does not fully constrain this form. Indeed, *decide* may be too strong a word, since the regime of truth offers a framework for the scene of recognition, delineating who will qualify as a subject of recognition and offering available norms for the act of recognition. In Foucault's view, there is always a relation to this regime, a mode of self-crafting that takes place in the context of the norms at issue and, specifically, negotiates an answer to the question of who the "I" will be in relation to these norms. In this sense, we are not deterministically decided by norms, although they do provide the framework and the point of reference for any set of decisions we subsequently make. This does not mean that a given regime of truth sets an invariable framework for recognition; it means only that it is in relation to this framework that recognition takes place or the norms that govern recognition are challenged and transformed.

His point, however, is not only that there is always a relation to such norms, but that any relation to the regime of truth will at the same time be a relation to myself. An operation of critique cannot take place without this reflexive dimension. To call into question a regime of truth, where that regime of truth governs subjectivation, is to call into question the truth of myself and, indeed, to question my ability to tell the truth about myself, to give an account of myself.

Thus if I question the regime of truth, I question, too, the regime through which being, and my own ontological status, is allocated. Critique is not merely *of* a given social practice or a certain horizon of intelligibility within which practices and institutions appear, it also implies that I come into question for myself. Self-questioning becomes an ethical consequence of critique for Foucault, as he makes clear in "What Is Critique?" It also turns out that self-questioning of this sort involves putting oneself at risk, imperiling the very possibility of being recognized by others, since to question the norms of recognition that govern what I might be, to ask what they leave out, what they might be compelled to accommodate, is, in relation to the present regime, to risk unrecognizability as a subject or at least to become an occasion for posing the questions of who one is (or can be) and whether or not one is recognizable.

These questions imply at least two kinds of inquiry for an ethical philosophy. First, what are these norms, to which my very being is given over, which have the power to install me or, indeed, to disinstall me as a recognizable subject? Second, where and who is this other, and can the notion of the other comprise the frame of reference and normative horizon that hold and confer my potential for becoming a recognizable subject? It seems right to fault Foucault for not making more room explicitly for the other in his consideration of ethics. Perhaps this is because the dyadic scene of self and other cannot describe adequately the social workings of normativity that condition both subject production and intersubjective exchange. If we conclude that Foucault's failure to think the other is decisive, we have perhaps overlooked the fact that the very being of the self is dependent, not just on the existence of the other in its singularity (as Levinas would have it), but also on the social dimension of normativity that governs the scene of recognition.[10] This social dimension of normativity precedes and conditions any dyadic exchange, even though it seems that we make contact with that sphere of normativity precisely in the context of such proximate exchanges.

The norms by which I recognize another or, indeed, myself are not mine alone. They function to the extent that they are social, exceeding every dyadic exchange that they condition. Their sociality, however, can be understood neither as a structuralist totality nor as a transcendental or quasi-transcendental invariability. Some would doubtless argue that norms must already be in place for recognition to become possible, and there is surely truth in such a claim. It is also true that certain practices of recognition or, indeed, certain breakdowns in the practice of recognition mark a site of rupture within the horizon of normativity and implicitly call for the institution of new norms, putting into question the givenness of the prevailing normative horizon. The normative horizon within which I see the other or, indeed, within which the other sees and listens and knows and recognizes is also subject to a critical opening.

It will not do, then, to collapse the notion of the other into the sociality of norms and claim that the other is implicitly present in the norms by which recognition is conferred. Sometimes the very unrecognizability of the other brings about a crisis in the norms that govern recognition. If and when, in an effort to confer or to receive a recognition that fails again and again, I call into question the normative horizon within which recognition takes place, this questioning is part of the desire for recognition, a desire that can find no satisfaction, and whose unsatisfiability establishes a critical point of departure for the interrogation of available norms.

In Foucault's view, this opening calls into question the limits of established regimes of truth, and there a certain risking of the self becomes, he claims, the sign of virtue.[11] What he does not say is that sometimes calling into question the regime of truth by which my own truth is established is motivated by the desire to recognize another or be recognized by one. The impossibility of doing so within the norms available to me compels me to adopt a critical relation to those norms. For Foucault, the regime of truth comes into question because "I" cannot recognize myself, or will not recognize myself, within the terms that are made available to me. In an effort to escape or overcome the terms by which subjectivation takes place, my struggle with norms is my own. His question effectively remains "Who can I be, given the regime of truth that determines ontology for me?" He does not ask the question "Who are you?" nor does he trace the way in which a critical perspective on norms might be elaborated starting out from either of those questions. Before we consider the consequences of this occlusion, let me suggest one final point about Foucault, although I will return to him later.

In asking the ethical question "How ought I to treat another?" I am immediately caught up in a realm of social normativity, since the other only appears to me, only functions as an other for me, if there is a frame within which I can see and apprehend the other in her separateness and exteriority. So, though I might think of the ethical relation as dyadic or, indeed, as presocial, I am caught up not only in the sphere of normativity but in the problematic of power when I pose the ethical question in its directness and simplicity: "How ought I to treat you?" If the "I" and the "you" must first come into being, and if a normative frame is necessary for this emergence and encounter, then norms work not only to direct my conduct but to condition the possible emergence of an encounter between myself and the other.

The first-person perspective assumed by the ethical question, as well as the direct address to a "you," are disoriented by this fundamental dependency of the ethical sphere on the social. Whether or not the other is singular, the other is recognized and confers recognition through a set of norms that govern recognizability. So, whereas the other may be singular, if not radically personal, the norms are to some extent impersonal and indifferent, and they introduce a disorientation of perspective for the subject in the midst of recognition as an encounter. If I understand myself to be conferring recognition on you, for instance, then I take seriously that the recognition comes from me. But the moment I realize that the terms by which I confer recognition are not mine alone, that I did not single-handedly devise or craft them, I am, as it were, dispossessed by the language that I offer. In a sense, I submit to a norm of recognition when I offer recognition to you, which means that the "I" is not offering this recognition from its own private resources. Indeed, it seems that the "I" is subjected to the norm at the moment it makes such an offering, so that the "I" becomes an instrument of that norm's agency. Thus the "I" seems invariably *used* by the norm to the degree that the "I" tries to use the norm. Though I thought I was having a relation to "you," I find that I am caught up in a struggle with norms. But could it also be true that I would not be in this struggle with norms if it were not for a desire to offer recognition to you? How do we understand this desire?

Post-Hegelian Queries:

> I can only recognize myself recognized by the other to the extent that this recognition of the other alters me: it is desire, it is what trembles in desire.
>
> —Jean-Luc Nancy, *The Restlessness of the Negative*

Perhaps the example I have just considered is misleading because, as Hegel would have it, recognition cannot be unilaterally given. In the moment that I give it, I am potentially given it, and the form in which I offer it is potentially given to me. This implied reciprocity is noted in *The Phenomenology of Spirit* when, in the section entitled "Lordship and Bondage," the first self-consciousness sees that it cannot have a unilateral effect on the other self-consciousness. Since they are structurally similar, the action of the one implies the action of the other. Self-consciousness learns this lesson first in the context of aggression toward the other, in a vain effort to destroy the structural similarity between the two and restore itself to a sovereign position: "this action of the one has itself the double significance of being both its own action and the action of the other as well. . . . Each sees the *other* do the same as it does; each does itself what it demands of the other, and therefore also does what it does only in so far as the other does the same."[12]

Similarly, when recognition becomes possible between these two vying subjects, it can never elude the structural condition of implicit reciprocity. One might say, then, that I can never offer recognition in the Hegelian sense as a pure offering, since I am receiving it, at least potentially and structurally, in the moment and in the act of giving. We might ask, as Levinas surely has of the Hegelian position, what kind of gift this is that returns to me so quickly, that never really leaves my hands. Does recognition, as Hegel argues, consist in a reciprocal act whereby I recognize that the other is structured in the same way I am? And do I recognize that the other also makes, or can make, this recognition of sameness? Or is there perhaps another encounter with alterity here that is irreducible to sameness? If it is the latter, how are we to understand this alterity?

The Hegelian other is always found outside; at least, it is *first* found outside and only later recognized to be constitutive of the subject. This has led some critics of Hegel to conclude that the Hegelian subject effects a wholesale assimilation of what is external into a set of features internal to itself, that its characteristic gesture is one of *appropriation* and its style that of imperialism. Other readings of Hegel, however, insist that the relation to the other is ecstatic,[13] that the "I" repeatedly finds itself outside itself, and that nothing can put an end to the repeated upsurge of this exteriority that is, paradoxically, my own. I am, as it were, always other to myself, and there is no final moment in which my return to myself takes place. In fact, if we are to follow *The Phenomenology of Spirit*, I am invariably transformed by the encounters I undergo; recognition becomes the process by which I become other than what I was and so cease to be able to return to what I was. There is, then, a constitutive loss in the process of recognition, since the "I" is transformed through the act of recognition. Not all of its past is gathered and known in the act of recognition; the act alters the organization of that past and its meaning at the same time that it transforms the present of the one who receives recognition. Recognition is an act in which the "return to self" becomes impossible for another reason as well. An encounter with an other effects a transformation of the self from which there is no return. What is recognized about a self in the course of this exchange is that the self is the sort of being for whom staying inside itself proves impossible. One is compelled and comported *outside oneself*; one finds that the only way to know oneself is through a mediation that takes place outside of oneself, exterior to oneself, by virtue of a convention or a norm that one did not make, in which one cannot discern oneself as an author or an agent of one's own making. In this sense, then, the Hegelian subject of recognition is one for whom a vacillation between loss and ecstasy is inevitable. The possibility of the "I," of speaking and knowing the "I," resides in a perspective that dislocates the first-person perspective it conditions.

The perspective that both conditions and disorients me from within the very possibility of my own perspective is not reducible to the perspective of the other, since this perspective also governs the possibility of my recognizing the other, and of the other's recognizing me. We are not mere dyads on our own, since our exchange is conditioned and mediated by language, by conventions, by a sedimentation of norms that are social in character and that exceed the perspective of those involved in the exchange. So how are we to understand the impersonal perspective by which our personal encounter is occasioned and disoriented?

Although Hegel is sometimes faulted for understanding recognition as a dyadic structure, we can see that within the *Phenomenology* the struggle for recognition is not the last word. It is important to see that the struggle for recognition as it is staged in the *Phenomenology* reveals the inadequacy of the dyad as a frame of reference for understanding social life. After all, what eventually follows from this scene is a system of customs (*Sittlichkeit*) and hence a social account of the norms by which reciprocal recognition might be sustained in ways that are more stable than either the life and death struggle or the system of bondage would imply.

The dyadic exchange refers to a set of norms that exceed the perspectives of those engaged in the struggle for recognition. When we ask what makes recognition possible, we find that it cannot merely be the other who is able to know and to recognize me as possessing a special talent or capacity, since that other will also have to rely, if only implicitly, upon certain criteria to establish what will and will not be recognizable about the self to anyone, a framework for seeing and judging who I am as well. In this sense, the other confers recognition—and we have yet to know precisely in what that consists—primarily by virtue of special internal capacities to discern who I may be, to read my face. If my face is readable at all, it becomes so only by entering into a visual frame that conditions its readability. If some can "read" me when others cannot, is it only because those who can read me have internal talents that others lack? Or is it that a certain practice of reading becomes possible in relation to certain frames and images that over time produce what we call "capacity"? For instance, if one is to respond ethically to a human face, there must first be a frame for the human, one that can include any number of variations as ready instances. But given how contested the visual representation of the 'human' is, it would appear that our capacity to respond to a face as a human face is conditioned and mediated by frames of reference that are variably humanizing and dehumanizing.

The possibility of an ethical response to the face thus requires a normativity of the visual field: there is already not only an epistemological frame within which the face appears, but an operation of power as well, since only by virtue of certain kinds of anthropocentric dispositions and cultural frames will a given face seem to be a human face to any one of us.[14] After all, under what conditions do some individuals acquire a face, a legible and visible face, and others do not? There is a language that frames the encounter, and embedded in that language is a set of norms concerning what will and will not constitute recognizability. This is Foucault's point and, in a way, his supplement to Hegel when he asks, "What can I become, given the contemporary order of being?" In "What Is Critique?" he writes, "What, therefore, am 'I,' I who belong to this humanity, perhaps to this piece of it, at this point in time, at this instant of humanity which is subjected to the power of truth in general and truths in particular?"[15] He understands that this "order" conditions the possibility of his becoming, and that a regime of truth, in his words, constrains what will and will not constitute the truth of his self, the truth he offers about himself, the truth by which he might be known and become recognizably human, the account he might give of himself.

"Who Are You?"

> You don't know me, anonymity insists. Now what?
>
> —Leigh Gilmore, *The Limits of Autobiography*

Though the social theory of recognition insists upon the impersonal operation of the norm in constituting the intelligibility of the subject, we nevertheless come into contact with these norms mainly through proximate and living exchanges, in the modes by which we are addressed and asked to take up the question of who we are and what our relation to the other ought to be. Given that these norms act upon us in the context of being addressed, the problem of singularity might provide a starting point for understanding the specific occasions of address through which these norms are appropriated in a living morality. In a Levinasian—though perhaps more decidedly Arendtian—vein, Adriana Cavarero argues that the question to ask is not "what" we are, as if the task were simply to fill in the content of our personhood. The question is not primarily a reflexive one, one that we pose to ourselves, as it is for Foucault, when he asks "What can I become?" For her, the very structure of address through which the question is posed gives us a clue to understanding its significance. The question most central to recognition is a direct one, and it is addressed to the other: "Who are you?" This question assumes that there is an other before us whom we do not know and cannot fully apprehend, one whose uniqueness and nonsubstitutability set a limit to the model of reciprocal recognition offered within the Hegelian scheme and to the possibility of knowing another more generally.

Cavarero underscores the kind of action that this speech act performs, grounding herself in an Arendtian conception of the social, which she mines for its ethical import. To this end, she cites Arendt's *Human Condition*: "Action and speech are so closely related because the primordial and specifically human act must at the same time answer to the question asked to every newcomer: 'who are you?' "[16]

In *Relating Narratives*, Cavarero offers a radically counter-Nietzschean approach to ethics in which, she claims, the question of the "who" engages the possibility of altruism. By the "question of the who" she does not mean the question "Who did this to whom?" that is, the question of strict moral accountability. Rather, it is a question that affirms that there is an other who is not fully known or knowable to me. In her chapter 2, Cavarero argues that Arendt focuses on a politics of "the who" in order to establish a relational politics, one in which the exposure and vulnerability of the other makes a primary ethical claim upon me (20–29).

In stark contrast to the Nietzschean view that life is essentially bound up with destruction and suffering, Cavarero argues that we are beings who are, of necessity, *exposed* to one another in our vulnerability and singularity, and that our political situation consists in part in learning how best to handle—and to honor—this constant and necessary exposure. In a sense, this theory of the "outside" to the subject radicalizes the ecstatic trend in the Hegelian position. In her view, I am not, as it were, an interior subject, closed upon myself, solipsistic, posing questions of myself alone. I exist in an important sense for you, and by virtue of you. If I have lost the conditions of address, if I have no "you" to address, then I have lost "myself." In her view, one can tell an autobiography only to an other, and one can reference an "I" only in relation to a "you": without the "you," my own story becomes impossible.

For Cavarero, this position implies a critique of conventional ways of understanding sociality, and in this sense she reverses the progression we saw in Hegel. Whereas *The Phenomenology of Spirit* moves from the scenario of the dyad toward a social theory of recognition, for Cavarero it is necessary to ground the social in the dyadic encounter. She writes:

> The "you" comes before the *we*, before the plural *you* and before the *they*. Symptomatically, the "you" is a term that is not at home in modern and contemporary developments of ethics and politics. The "you" is ignored by individualistic doctrines, which are too preoccupied with praising the rights of the *I*, and the "you" is masked by a Kantian form of ethics that is only capable of staging an *I* that addresses itself as a familiar "you." Neither does the "you" find a home in the schools of thought to which individualism is opposed—these schools reveal themselves for the most part to be affected by a moralistic vice, which, in order to avoid falling into the decadence of the *I*, avoids the contiguity of the *you*, and privileges collective, plural pronouns. Indeed, many revolutionary movements (which range from traditional communism to the feminism of sisterhood) seem to share a curious linguistic code based on the intrinsic morality of pronouns. The *we* is always positive, the *plural you* is a possible ally, the *they* has the face of an antagonist, the *I* is unseemly, and the *you* is, of course, superfluous. (90–91)

For Cavarero, the "I" encounters not only this or that attribute of the other, but the fact of this other as fundamentally exposed, visible, seen, existing in a bodily way and of necessity in a domain of appearance. *This* exposure that I am constitutes, as it were, my singularity. I cannot will it away, for it is a feature of my very corporeality and, in this sense, of my life. Yet it is not that over which I can have control. One might borrow from Heideggerian parlance to explain Cavarero's view and say that no one can be exposed for me, and I am, in this way, nonsubstitutable. But does the social theory derived from Hegel, in its insistence on the impersonal perspective of the norm, counter by establishing my substitutability after all? Am I, in relation to the norm, substitutable? And yet, as a being constituted bodily in the public sphere, argues Cavarero, I am exposed and singular, and this is as much a part of my publicity, if not my sociality, as is the way I become recognizable through the operation of norms.

Cavarero's argument both undercuts the Nietzschean account of aggression and punishment and limits the claims of Hegelian sociality upon us; it also offers direction for a different theory of recognition. There are at least two points to be made here. The first has to do with our fundamental dependency on the other, the fact that we cannot exist without addressing the other and without being addressed by the other, and that there is no wishing away our fundamental sociality. (You can see that I resort here to the plural *we*, even though Cavarero advises against it, precisely because I am not convinced that we must abandon it.) The second point limits the first. No matter how much we each desire recognition and require it, we are not therefore the same as the other, and not everything counts as recognition in the same way. Although I have argued that no one can recognize another simply by virtue of special psychological or critical skills and that norms condition the possibility of recognition, it still matters that we feel more properly recognized by some people than we do by others. And this difference cannot be explained solely through recourse to the notion that the norm operates variably. Cavarero argues for an irreducibility to each of our beings that becomes clear in the distinct stories we have to tell, so that any effort to identify fully with a collective "we" will necessarily fail. As Cavarero puts it:

> what we have called an altruistic ethics of relation does not support empathy, identification, or confusions. Rather this ethic desires a *you* that is truly an other, in her uniqueness and distinction. No matter how much you are similar and consonant, says this ethic, your story is never my story. No matter how much the larger traits of our life-stories are similar, I still do not recognize myself *in* you and, even less, in the collective *we*. (92)

The uniqueness of the other is exposed to me, but mine is also exposed to her. This does not mean we are the same, but only that we are bound to one another by what differentiates us, namely, our singularity. The notion of singularity is very often bound up with existential romanticism and with a claim of authenticity, but I gather that, precisely because it is without content, my singularity has some properties in common with yours and so is, to some extent, a substitutable term. In other words, even as Cavarero argues that singularity sets a limit to substitutability, she also argues that singularity has no defining content other than the irreducibility of exposure, of being *this* body exposed to a publicity that is variably and alternately intimate and anonymous. Hegel analyzes the "this" in the *Phenomenology*, pointing out that it never specifies without generalizing, that the term, in its very substitutability, undercuts the specificity it seeks to indicate: "When I say: 'a single thing,' I am really saying what it is from a wholly universal point of view, for everything is a single thing; and likewise 'this thing' is anything you like. If we describe it more exactly as 'this bit of paper,' then each and every bit of paper is 'this bit of paper,' and I have only uttered the universal all the time."[17] Insofar as "this" fact of singularizing exposure, which follows from bodily existence, is one that can be reiterated endlessly, it constitutes a collective condition, characterizing us all equally, not only reinstalling the "we," but also establishing a structure of substitutability at the core of singularity.

One may think that this conclusion is too happily Hegelian, but I would like to interrogate it further, since I think it has ethical consequences for the problem of giving an account of oneself for another. This exposure, for instance, cannot be narrated. I cannot give an account of it, even though it structures any account I might give. The norms by which I seek to make myself recognizable are not fully mine. They are not born with me; the temporality of their emergence does not coincide with the temporality of my own life. So, in living my life as a recognizable being, I live a vector of temporalities, one of which has my death as its terminus, but another of which consists in the social and historical temporality of the norms by which my recognizability is established and maintained. These norms are, as it were, indifferent to me, to my life and my death. Because norms emerge, transform, and persist according to a temporality that is not the same as the temporality of my life, and because they also in some ways sustain my life in its intelligibility, the temporality of norms interrupts the time of my living. Paradoxically, it is this interruption, this disorientation of the perspective of my life, this instance of an indifference in sociality, that nevertheless sustains my living.

Foucault put this point dramatically in his essay "Politics and the Study of Discourse" when he wrote, "I know as well as anyone how 'thankless' such research can be, how irritating it is to approach discourses not by way of the gentle, silent and intimate consciousness which expresses itself through them, but through an obscure set of anonymous rules." He continues, "Must I suppose that, in my discourse, it is not my own survival that is at stake? And that, by speaking, I do not exorcise my death, but establish it; or rather, that I suppress all interiority, and yield my utterance to an outside which is so indifferent to my life, so *neutral*, that it knows no difference between my life and my death?" These rhetorical questions mark a sense of inevitability in the face of the fact that one's own life cannot be redeemed or extended through discourse (even though they tacitly praise discourse as that which finally has a life that is more robust than our own). For those who believe that language houses an intimate subjectivity whose death is overcome there as well, Foucault writes, "they cannot bear—and one can understand them a little—to be told: discourse is not life; its time is not yours."[18]

So the account of myself that I give in discourse never fully expresses or carries this living self. My words are taken away as I give them, interrupted by the time of a discourse that is not the same as the time of my life. This "interruption" contests the sense of the account's being grounded in myself alone, since the indifferent structures that enable my living belong to a sociality that exceeds me.

Indeed, this interruption and dispossession of my perspective *as mine* can take place in different ways. There is the operation of a norm, invariably social, that conditions what will and will not be a recognizable account, exemplified in the fact that I am used by the norm precisely to the degree that I use it. And there can be no account of myself that does not, to some extent, conform to norms that govern the humanly recognizable, or that negotiate these terms in some ways, with various risks following from that negotiation. But, as I will try to explain later, it is also the case that I give an account *to* someone, and that the addressee of the account, real or imaginary, also functions to interrupt the sense that this account of myself is my own. If it is an account of myself, and it is an accounting *to* someone, then I am compelled to give the account away, to send it off, to be dispossessed of it at the very moment that I establish it as *my* account. No account takes place outside the structure of address, even if the addressee remains implicit and unnamed, anonymous and unspecified. The address establishes the account as an account, and so the account is completed only on the occasion when it is effectively exported and expropriated from the domain of what is my own. It is only in dispossession that I can and do give any account of myself.

If I try to give an account of myself, if I try to make myself recognizable and understandable, then I might begin with a narrative account of my life. But this narrative will be disoriented by what is not mine, or not mine alone. And I will, to some degree, have to make myself substitutable in order to make myself recognizable. The narrative authority of the "I" must give way to the perspective and temporality of a set of norms that contest the singularity of my story.

We can surely still tell our stories, and there will be many reasons to do precisely that. But we will not be able to be very authoritative when we try to give a full account with a narrative structure. The "I" can tell neither the story of its own emergence nor the conditions of its own possibility without bearing witness to a state of affairs to which one could not have been present, which are prior to one's own emergence as a subject who can know, and so constitute a set of origins that one can narrate only at the expense of authoritative knowledge. Narration is surely possible under such circumstances, but it is, as Thomas Keenan has pointed out, surely fabulous.[19] Fictional narration in general requires no referent to work as narrative, and we might say that the irrecoverability and foreclosure of the referent is the very condition of possibility for an account of myself, if that account is to take narrative form. The irrecoverability of an original referent does not destroy narrative; it produces it "in a fictional direction," as Lacan would say. So to be more precise, I would have to say that I can tell the story of my origin and I can even tell it again and again, in several ways. But the story of my origin I tell is not one for which I am accountable, and it cannot establish my accountability. At least, let's hope not, since, over wine usually, I tell it in various ways, and the accounts are not always consistent with one another. Indeed, it may be that to have an origin means precisely to have several possible versions of the origin—I take it that this is part of what Nietzsche meant by the operation of genealogy. Any one of those is a possible narrative, but of no single one can I say with certainty that it alone is true.

Indeed, I can try to give narrative form to certain conditions of my emergence, try, as it were, to tell a story about what meanings "exposure to the other" may have had for me, what it was to be this emergent body in that intimate or public sphere, try to tell a story about norms in discourse as well—when and where I learned them, what I thought of them, which ones became incorporated at once, and in what way. At this point the story that I tell, one that may even have a certain necessity, cannot assume that its referent adequately takes narrative form,[20] since the exposure I seek to narrate is also the precondition of that narration, a facticity, as it were, that cannot yield to narrative form. And if I tell the story to a "you," that other is implied not only as an internal feature of the narrative but also as an irreducibly exterior condition and trajectory of the mode of address.

There are, then, several ways in which the account I may give of myself has the potential to break apart and to become undermined. My efforts to give an account of myself founder in part because I *address* my account, and in addressing my account I am exposed to you. Can I take account of this very exposure implied by address in the course of my narrative? This exposure takes place in spoken language and, in a different way, in written address as well, but I am not sure I can give an account of it.[21] Is it there, as it were, as a condition of my narration, one I cannot fully thematize within any narrative I might provide, one that does not fully yield to a sequential account? There is a bodily referent here, a condition of me that I can point to, but that I cannot narrate precisely, even though there are no doubt stories about where my body went and what it did and did not do. The stories do not capture the body to which they refer. Even the history of this body is not fully narratable. To be a body is, in some sense, to be deprived of having a full recollection of one's life. There is a history to my body of which I can have no recollection.

If there is, then, a part of bodily experience as well—of what is indexed by the word *exposure*—that cannot be narrated but constitutes the bodily condition of one's narrative account of oneself, then exposure constitutes one among several vexations in the effort to give a narrative account of oneself. There is (1) a non-narrativizable *exposure* that establishes my singularity, and there are (2) *primary relations*, irrecoverable, that form lasting and recurrent impressions in the history of my life, and so (3) a history that establishes my *partial* opacity to myself. Lastly, there are (4) *norms* that facilitate my telling about myself but that I do not author and that render me substitutable at the very moment that I seek to establish the history of my singularity. This last dispossession in language is intensified by the fact that I give an account of myself to someone, so that the narrative structure of my account is superseded by (5) the *structure of address* in which it takes place.

Exposure, like the operation of the norm, constitutes the conditions of my own emergence as a reflective being, one with memory, one who might be said to have a story to tell (these postulates from both Nietzsche and Freud can be accepted, even if the formative role of punishment and morality in their accounts is disputed). Accordingly, I cannot be present to a temporality that precedes my own capacity for self-reflection, and whatever story about myself that I might give has to take this constitutive incommensurability into consideration. It constitutes the way in which my story arrives belatedly, missing some of the constitutive beginnings and the preconditions of the life it seeks to narrate. This means that my narrative begins *in media res*, when many things have already taken place to make me and my story possible in language. I am always recuperating, reconstructing, and I am left to fictionalize and fabulate origins I cannot know. In the making of the story, I create myself in new form, instituting a narrative "I" that is superadded to the "I" whose past life I seek to tell. The narrative "I" effectively adds to the story every time it tries to speak, since the "I" appears again as the narrative perspective, and this addition cannot be fully narrated at the moment in which it provides the perspectival anchor for the narration in question.

My account of myself is partial, haunted by that for which I can devise no definitive story. I cannot explain exactly why I have emerged in this way, and my efforts at narrative reconstruction are always undergoing revision. There is that in me and of me for which I can give no account. But does this mean that I am not, in the moral sense, accountable for who I am and for what I do? If I find that, despite my best efforts, a certain opacity persists and I cannot make myself fully accountable to you, is this ethical failure? Or is it a failure that gives rise to another ethical disposition in the place of a full and satisfying notion of narrative accountability? Is there in this affirmation of partial transparency a possibility for acknowledging a relationality that binds me more deeply to language and to you than I previously knew? And is the relationality that conditions and blinds this "self" not, precisely, an indispensable resource for ethics?

Against Ethical Violence

> While I can't believe in a selfhood which is any other than generated by language
> over time, I can still lack conviction if I speak of myself in the necessarily settled
> language of a sociologised subject. This self-describing "I" produces an unease which
> can't be mollified by any theory of its constructed nature. . . . What purports to be
> "I" speaks back to me, and I can't quite believe what I hear it say.
>
> —Denise Riley, *The Words of Selves*

An ability to affirm what is contingent and incoherent in oneself may allow one to affirm others who may or may not "mirror" one's own constitution. There is, after all, always the tacit operation of the mirror in Hegel's concept of reciprocal recognition, since I must somehow see that the other is like me, and see that the other is making the same recognition of our likeness. There is lots of light in the Hegelian room, and the mirrors have the happy coincidence of usually being windows, as well.[1] This view of recognition does not encounter an exteriority that resists a bad infinity of recursive mimesis. There is no opacity that shadows these windows or dims that light. In consequence, we might consider a certain post-Hegelian reading of the scene of recognition in which precisely my own opacity to myself occasions my capacity to confer a certain kind of recognition on others. It would be, perhaps, an ethics based on our shared, invariable, and partial blindness about ourselves. The recognition that one is, at every turn, not quite the same as how one presents oneself in the available discourse might imply, in turn, a certain patience with others that would suspend the demand that they be self-same at every moment. Suspending the demand for self-identity or, more particularly, for complete coherence seems to me to counter a certain ethical violence, which demands that we manifest and maintain self-identity at all times and require that others do the same. For subjects who invariably live within a temporal horizon, this is a difficult, if not impossible, norm to satisfy. The capacity of a subject to recognize and become recognized is occasioned by a normative discourse whose temporality is not the same as a first-person perspective. This temporality of discourse disorients one's own. Thus, it follows that one can give and take recognition only on the condition that one becomes disoriented from oneself by something which is not oneself, that one undergoes a de-centering and "fails" to achieve self-identity.

Can a new sense of ethics emerge from such inevitable ethical failure? I suggest that it can, and that it would be spawned by a certain willingness to acknowledge the limits of acknowledgment itself. When we claim to know and to present ourselves, we will fail in some ways that are nevertheless essential to who we are. We cannot reasonably expect anything different from others in return. To acknowledge one's own opacity or that of another does not transform opacity into transparency. To know the limits of acknowledgment is to know even this fact in a limited way; as a result, it is to experience the very limits of knowing. This can, by the way, constitute a disposition of humility and generosity alike: I will need to be forgiven for what I cannot have fully known, and I will be under a similar obligation to offer forgiveness to others, who are also constituted in partial opacity to themselves.

If the identity we say we are cannot possibly capture us and marks immediately an excess and opacity that falls outside the categories of identity, then any effort "to give an account of oneself" will have to fail in order to approach being true. As we ask to know the other, or ask that the other say, finally or definitively, who he or she is, it will be important not to expect an answer that will ever satisfy. By not pursuing satisfaction and by letting the question remain open, even enduring, we let the other live, since life might be understood as precisely that which exceeds any account we may try to give of it. If letting the other live is part of any ethical definition of recognition, then this version of recognition will be based less on knowledge than on an apprehension of epistemic limits.

In a sense, the ethical stance consists, as Cavarero suggests, in asking the question "Who are you?" and continuing to ask it without any expectation of a full or final answer. The other to whom I pose this question will not be captured by any answer that might arrive to satisfy it. So if there is, in the question, a desire for recognition, this desire will be under an obligation to keep itself alive as desire and not to resolve itself. "Oh, now I know who you are": at this moment, I cease to address you, or to be addressed by you. Lacan infamously cautioned, "do not cede upon your desire."[2] This is an ambiguous claim, since he does not say that your desire should or must be satisfied. He says only that desire should not be stopped. Indeed, sometimes satisfaction is the very means by which one cedes upon desire, the means by which one turns against it, arranging for its quick death.

Hegel was the one who linked desire to recognition, providing the formulation that was recast by Hyppolite as the desire to desire. And it was in the context of Hyppolite's seminar that Lacan was exposed to this formulation. Although Lacan would argue that misrecognition is a necessary byproduct of desire, it may be that an account of recognition, in all its errancy, can still work in relation to the problem of desire. To revise recognition as an ethical project, we will need to see it as, in principle, unsatisfiable. For Hegel, it is important to remember, the desire to be, the desire to persist in one's own being—a doctrine first articulated by Spinoza in his *Ethics*—is fulfilled only through the desire *to be recognized*.[3] But if recognition works to capture or arrest desire, then what has happened to the desire to be and to persist in one's own being? Spinoza marks for us the desire to live, to persist, upon which any theory of recognition is built. And because the terms by which recognition operates may seek to fix and capture us, they run the risk of arresting desire, and of putting an end to life. As a result, it is important for ethical philosophy to consider that any theory of recognition will have to give an account of the desire for recognition, remembering that desire sets the limits and the conditions for the operation of recognition itself. Indeed, a certain desire to persist, we might say, following Spinoza, under-writes recognition, so that forms of recognition or, indeed, forms of judgment that seek to relinquish or destroy the desire to persist, the desire for life itself, undercut the very preconditions of recognition.

Limits of Judgment

> I can't help but dream about a criticism that would try not to judge but to bring an *oeuvre*, a book, a sentence, an idea to life. . . . It would multiply not judgments but signs of life.
>
> —Michel Foucault, "The Masked Philosopher"

Recognition cannot be reduced to making and delivering judgments about others. Indisputably, there are ethical and legal situations where such judgments must be made. We should not, however, con-clude that the legal determination of guilt or innocence is the same as social recognition. In fact, recognition sometimes obligates us to suspend judgment in order to apprehend the other. We sometimes rely on judgments of guilt or innocence to summarize another's life, confusing the ethical posture with the one that judges.[4] To what extent is the scene of recognition presupposed by the act of judg-ment? And does recognition provide a broader framework within which moral judgment itself might be assessed? Is it still possible to ask the question "What is the value of moral judgment?" And can we ask this in a way that recalls Nietzsche's question "What is the *value* of morality?" When Nietzsche posed this question, he also implicitly accorded value to the question he posed. That question presupposes that if there is a value to morality, we find it outside of morality itself, an extra-moral value by which we gauge morality, thus asserting that morality does not exhaustively comprise the field of values.

The scene of moral judgment, when it is a judgment of persons for being as they are, invariably establishes a clear moral distance between the one who judges and the one who is judged. If you consider, however, Simone de Beauvoir's question "Must we burn Sade?" matters become more complicated. It may be that only through an experience of the other under conditions of suspended judgment do we finally become capable of an ethical reflection on the humanity of the other, even when that other has sought to annihilate humanity.[5] Although I am certainly not arguing that we ought never to make judgments—they are urgently necessary for political, legal, and personal life alike—I think that it is important, in rethinking the cultural terms of ethics, to remember that not all ethical relations are reducible to acts of judgment and that the very capacity to judge presupposes a prior relation between those who judge and those who are judged. The capacity to make and justify moral judgments does not exhaust the sphere of ethics and is not coextensive with ethical obligation or ethical relationality. Moreover, judgment, as important as it is, cannot qualify as a theory of recognition; indeed, we may well judge another without recognizing him or her at all.

Prior to judging an other, we must be in some relation to him or her. This relation will ground and inform the ethical judgments we finally do make. We will, in some way, have to ask the question "Who are you?" If we forget that we are related to those we condemn, even those we *must* condemn, then we lose the chance to be ethically educated or "addressed" by a consideration of who they are and what their personhood says about the range of human possibility that exists, even to prepare ourselves for or against such possibilities.

We also forget that judging another is a mode of address: even punishments are pronounced, and often delivered, to the face of the other, requiring that other's bodily presence. *Hence, if there is an ethic to the address, and if judgment, including legal judgment, is one form of address, then the ethical value of judgment will be conditioned by the form of address it takes.*

Consider that one way we become responsible and self-knowing is facilitated by a kind of reflection that takes place when judgments are suspended. Condemnation, denunciation, and excoriation work as quick ways to posit an ontological difference between judge and judged, even to purge oneself of another. Condemnation becomes the way in which we establish the other as nonrecognizable or jettison some aspect of ourselves that we lodge in the other, whom we then condemn. In this sense, condemnation can work against self-knowledge, inasmuch as it moralizes a self by disavowing commonality with the judged. Although self-knowledge is surely limited, that is not a reason to turn against it as a project. Condemnation tends to do precisely this, to purge and externalize one's own opacity. In this sense, judgment can be a way to fail to own one's limitations and thus provides no felicitous basis for a reciprocal recognition of human beings as opaque to themselves, partially blind, constitutively limited. To know oneself as limited is still to know something about oneself, even if one's knowing is afflicted by the limitation that one knows.

Similarly, condemnation is very often an act that not only "gives up on" the one condemned but seeks to inflict a violence upon the condemned in the name of "ethics." Kafka offers several instances of how this kind of ethical violence works. Take, for example, the fate of Georg in the story called "The Judgment."[6] His father condemns him to death by drowning, and Georg is rushed from the room, as if by the force of the utterance itself, and over the side of the bridge. Of course, that utterance has to appeal to a psyche disposed to satisfy the father's wish to see the son dead, as the verb tenses in the story also confirm, so the condemnation cannot work unilaterally. Georg must take the condemnation as the principle of his own conduct and participate in the will that rushes him from the room.

It is unclear in Kafka's story whether the characters are separate entities or function as porously partitioned parts of a self that is no entity, bears no core, constituted only within a field of fragmentation. The son claims to have a friend who turns out to be, perhaps, no more than an imaginary mirror-fragment of himself. The father claims to have written to this friend, and it is finally unclear whether the friend even exists or whether he is the point of struggle between what belongs to the father and what to the son. The friend is the name for a boundary that is never fully clear. When the father condemns the son, the father himself collapses on the bed with a large sound, as if the condemnation had struck him down, as well. After the father declares, "I sentence you [*verurteile dich*] to death by drowning!" Georg is said to have "felt himself rushed [*fühlte sich . . . gejagt*] from the room, the crash with which his father fell on the bed behind him was still in his ears as he fled." It seems as if the father, in condemning the son, also condemned himself. By the next sentence, Georg is described as having "rushed [*eilte*] down" the steps and "rushed [*sprang*]" out the door and "across the roadway, driven [*triebt es ihn*] towards the water." He rushes, the subject of an active verb, but he is also "driven," the accusative object of an action precipitated from elsewhere. To understand his agency in this scene of fatal condemnation, one would have to accept the simultaneity of both conditions: *being driven, rushing himself. Triebt es ihn* suggests that "it" drives him, but what is this impersonal "it," which seems to be neither clearly the father's will nor his own, a term that marks the equivocation between the two that drives, as it were, the entire story? At the end of the line, Georg will have fulfilled his father's demand, and though we might conjecture that Georg does this to secure his father's love, he seems rather to avow the unilateral nature of his own love for his parents.

What begins as a paternal condemnation now takes shape as the prospect of the son's urgent need about to be satisfied. "Already he was grasping at the railings as a starving man clutches food (*die Nah-rung*)." When Georg swings himself over the rails, he is likened to "the distinguished gymnast he had once been in his youth, to his parents' pride." Although the strong wind of the father's condemnation forces Georg out of the room and down the stairs, the suicidal acrobatics that he performs are his own voluntary action, one performed *for* the father, recreating the imaginary scene of approval and avowing his love for his father at the very moment he complies with the death edict. Indeed, his self-destruction seems to be offered as a final gift of love. Georg waits to let himself fall until he "spies a motor bus coming which would easily cover the noise of his fall." And his final words, delivered in a "low voice"—to make sure his death remains inaudible—are "dear parents, I have always loved you, all the same [*Liebe Eltern, ich habe euch doch immer geliebt*]." The translation of *doch* as "all the same" is perhaps stronger than it need be. There is in the *doch* a certain protest and rebuttal, an "even though" or, better, a "still." Some difficulty is obliquely referenced by this single word, but it hardly rises to the level of a counter-accusation.

Georg's confession of love for his parents seems to be less an act of forgiveness than a semi-blissful spectacle of masochism. He dies for their sins, and the charwoman who passes him on the stairs cries "Jesus!" and covers her eyes when she sees him. Georg's words of love for his parents seem essential to the execution of the death sentence. His utterance seals and effects the condemnation. The reflexive action of "letting himself drop [*liess sich hinabfallen*]" is nothing more than a deadly way of consecrating his attachment to his parents. His death becomes a gift of love. Although the father's utterance seems to initiate the act, the acrobatics are surely Georg's own, so the action of the former transmutes quite smoothly into the action of the latter. Georg dies not only because his brutal father demands that he die but because his father's demand has become the perverse nourishment of his life.

Georg's suicidal fidelity, however, does not take away from the fact that if condemnation does seek, in the extreme, to annihilate the other, then the extreme version of punishing condemnation is the death sentence. In more ameliorated forms, the condemnation still takes aim at the life of the condemned, destroying his ethical capacity. If it is a life that must be demeaned and destroyed rather than, say, a set of acts, punishment works to further destroy the conditions for autonomy, eroding if not eviscerating the capacity of the subject addressed for both self-reflection and social recognition, two practices that are, I would argue, essential to any substantive account of ethical life. It also, of course, turns the moralist into a murderer.

When denunciation works to paralyze and deratify the critical capacities of the subject to whom it is delivered, it undermines or even destroys the very capacities that are needed for ethical reflection and conduct, sometimes leading to suicidal conclusions. This suggests that recognition must be sustained for ethical judgment to work productively. In other words, for judgment to inform the self-reflective deliberations of a subject who stands a chance of acting differently in the future, it must work in the service of sustaining and promoting life. Such a conception of punishment differs drastically from the Nietzschean account we considered earlier.

In a real sense, we do not survive without being addressed, which means that the scene of address can and should provide a sustaining condition for ethical deliberation, judgment, and conduct. In the same way, I would argue, the institutions of punishment and imprisonment have a responsibility to sustain the very lives that enter their domains, precisely because they have the power, in the name of "ethics," to damage and destroy lives with impunity. If, as Spinoza maintained, one can desire to live life in the right way only if there is, already or at the same time, a desire to live, it would seem equally true that the scenario of punishment that seeks to transform the desire for life into a desire for death erodes the condition of ethics itself.

Psychoanalysis

> *Cressida*: Stop my mouth. . . .
>   I know not what I speak.
>
> —Shakespeare, *The History of Troilus and Cressida*

How do these concerns relate to the question of whether one can give an account of oneself? Let us remember that one gives an account of oneself to another, and that every accounting takes place within a scene of address. I give an account of myself *to you*. Furthermore, the scene of address, what we might call the rhetorical condition for responsibility, means that while I am engaging in a reflexive activity, thinking about and reconstructing myself, I am also speaking to you and thus elaborating a relation to an other in language as I go. The ethical valence of the situation is thus not restricted to the question of whether or not my account of myself is adequate, but rather concerns whether, in giving the account, I establish a relationship to the one to whom my account is addressed and whether both parties to the interlocution are sustained and altered by the scene of address.

Within the context of the psychoanalytic transference, the "you" is often a default structure of address, the elaboration of a "you" in an imaginary domain, and an address through which prior, and more archaic, forms of address are conveyed.[7] In the transference, speech sometimes works to convey information (including information about my life), but it also functions as both the conduit for a desire and a rhetorical instrument that seeks to alter or act upon the interlocutory scene itself.[8] Psychoanalysis has always understood this dual dimension of the self-disclosing speech act. On the one hand, it is an effort to communicate information about oneself; yet, on the other hand, it recreates and constitutes anew the tacit presumptions about communication and relationality that structure the mode of address. Transference is thus the recreation of a primary relationality within the analytic space, one that potentially yields a new or altered relationship (and capacity for relationality) on the basis of analytic work.

Narrative functions within the context of the transference not only a means by which information is conveyed but as a rhetorical deployment of language that seeks to *act upon* the other, motivated by a desire or wish that assumes an allegorical form in the interlocutory scene of the analysis. The "I" is narrated but also posited and articulated within the context of the scene of address. What is produced in discourse often confounds the intentional aims of speaking. The "you" is variable and imaginary at the same time as it is bounded, recalcitrant, and stubbornly there. The "you" constitutes an object in relation to which an aim of desire becomes articulable, but what recurs in this relation to the other, this scene for the articulation of desire, is an opacity that is not fully "illuminated" through speech. So "I" tell a story to "you," and we might together consider the details of the story that I tell. But if I tell them to you in the context of a transference (and can there be telling without transference?), I am doing something with this telling, acting on you in some way. And this telling is also doing something to me, acting on me, in ways that I may well not understand as I go.

Within some psychoanalytic circles, doctrines, and practices, one of the stated aims of psychoanalysis is to offer the client the chance to put together a story about herself, to recollect the past, to interweave the events or, rather, the wishes of childhood with later events, to try to make sense through narrative means of what this life has been, the impasses it encounters time and again, and what it might yet become. Indeed, some have argued that the normative goal of psychoanalysis is to permit the client to tell a single and coherent story about herself that will satisfy the wish to know herself, moreover, to know herself in part through a narrative reconstruction in which the interventions by the analyst or therapist contribute in many ways to the remaking and reweaving of the story. Roy Schafer has argued this position, and we see it in several versions of psychoanalytic practice described by clinicians in scholarly and popular venues.[9]

But what if the narrative reconstruction of a life *cannot* be the goal of psychoanalysis, and that the reason for this has to do with the very formation of the subject? If the other is always there, from the start, in the place of where the ego will be, then a life is constituted through a fundamental interruption, is even *interrupted prior to the possibility of any continuity*. Accordingly, if narrative reconstruction is to approximate the life it means to convey, it must also be subject to interruption. Of course, learning to construct a narrative is a crucial practice, especially when discontinuous bits of experience remain dissociated from one another by virtue of traumatic conditions. And I do not mean to undervalue the importance of narrative work in the reconstruction of a life that otherwise suffers from fragmentation and discontinuity. The suffering that belongs to conditions of dissociation should not be underestimated. Conditions of hyper-mastery, however, are no more salutary than conditions of radical fragmentation. It seems true that we might well need a narrative to connect parts of the psyche and experience that cannot be assimilated to one another. But too much connection can lead to extreme forms of paranoid isolation. In any event, it does not follow that, if a life needs some narrative structure, then all of life must be rendered in narrative form. That conclusion would transform a minimum requirement of psychic stability into the principle aim of analytic work.

What is left out if we assume, as some do, that narrative gives us the life that is ours, or that life takes place in narrative form? The "mineness" of a life is not necessarily its story form. The "I" who begins to tell its story can tell it only according to recognizable norms of life narration. We might then say: to the extent that the "I" agrees, from the start, to narrate itself through those norms, it agrees to circuit its narration through an externality, and so to disorient itself in the telling through modes of speech that have an impersonal nature.[10] Of course, Lacan has made clear that whatever account is given about the primary inaugural moments of a subject is belated and phantasmatic, affected irreversibly by a *nachträglichkeit*. Developmental narratives tend to err by assuming that the narrator of such a narrative can be present to the origins of the story. The origin is made available only retroactively, and through the screen of fantasy. The mental health norm that tells us that giving a coherent account of oneself is part of the ethical labor of psychoanalysis misconstrues what psychoanalysis can and must do. In fact, it subscribes to an account of the subject that belies part of the very ethical significance of that subject's formation.

If I give an account, and give it to you, then my narrative depends upon a structure of address. But if I can address you, I must first have been addressed, brought into the structure of address as a possibility of language before I was able to find my own way to make use of it. This follows, not only from the fact that language first belongs to the other and I acquire it through a complicated form of mimesis, but also because the very possibility of linguistic agency is derived from the situation in which one finds oneself addressed by a language one never chose. If I am first addressed by another, and if this address comes to me prior to my individuation, in what forms then does it come to me? It would seem that one is always addressed in one way or another, even if one is abandoned or abused, since the void and the injury hail one in specific ways.

This view has disparate philosophical and psychoanalytic formulations. Levinas has claimed that the address of the other constitutes me and that this seizure by the other precedes any formation of the self (*le Moi*). Jean Laplanche, in a psychoanalytic vein, argues something similar when he claims that the address of the other, conceived as a demand, implants or insinuates itself into what will later come to be called, in a theoretical vein, "my unconscious."[11] In a sense, this nomenclature will always be giving the lie to itself. It will be impossible to speak without error of "my unconscious" because it is not a possession, but rather that which I cannot own. And yet the

grammar by which we seek to give an account of this psychic domain, which I do not, and cannot, own, paradoxically attributes this
unconscious to me, as that which belongs to me as a predicate of the
subject, just as any number of other features might be said to belong
to me, the grammatical and ontological subject. To understand the
unconscious, however, is to understand what *cannot* belong, properly
speaking, to me, precisely because it defies the rhetoric of belonging,
is a way of being dispossessed through the address of the other from
the start. For Laplanche, I am animated by this call or demand, and
I am at first overwhelmed by it. The other is, from the start, too
much for me, enigmatic, inscrutable. This "too-much-ness" must be
handled and contained for something called an "I" to emerge in its
separateness. The unconscious is not a topos into which this "too
much-ness" is deposited. It is rather formed as a psychic requirement
of survival and individuation, as a way of managing—and failing to
manage—that excess and thus as the persistent and opaque life of
that excess itself.

The transference is precisely the emotionally laden scene of address, recalling the other and its overwhelmingness, rerouting the
unconscious through an externality from whom it is returned in some
way. So the point of the transference and the counter-transference is
not only to build or rebuild the story of one's life but also to enact
what cannot be narrated, and to enact the unconscious as it is relived
in the scene of address itself. If the transference recapitulates the
unconscious, then I undergo a dispossession of myself in the scene
of address. This does not mean that I am possessed by the other,
since the other is also dispossessed, called upon, and calling, in a
relation that is not, for that reason, reciprocal. Nevertheless, just
because the analyst (hopefully) handles this dispossession better than
I do, there is a dislocation that both interlocutors undergo for access
to the unconscious to take place. I am caught up in that address,
even as the analyst contracts not to overwhelm me with her need.
Nevertheless, I am overwhelmed by something, and I think I am

overwhelmed by her; she is the name I have for this "too-much-ness." But what does she name?

In this context the question of the "who" reemerges: "By whom am I overwhelmed?" "Who is she?" "Who are you?" are all, in a sense, the question the infant poses to demands of the adult: "Who are you, and what do you want of me?" In this respect, Laplanche's perspective offers us a way of revising Cavarero's claim that the question that inaugurates ethics is "Who are you?" When the analyst is the other, I cannot know who the other is, but the pursuit of this unsatisfiable question elaborates the ways in which an enigmatic other, understood as the variegated demands of the adult world, inaugurates and structures me. It also means that she occupies a position for me as both more and less than what she is, and this incommensurability between the analyst as, say, person, and the analyst as, say, occasion for my psychic material lays the groundwork for the contribution that the client makes to the transferential scene. The analyst is, in her own way, dispossessed in the moment of acting as its site of transfer for me, and for reasons that I cannot know. What am I calling on her to be? And how does she take up that call? What my call recalls for her will be the site of the counter-transference, but about this I can have only the most refracted knowledge. Vainly I ask, "Who are you?" and then, more soberly, "What have I become here?" And she asks those questions of me as well, from her own distance, and in ways I cannot precisely know or hear. This not-knowing draws upon a prior not-knowing, the one by which the subject is inaugurated, although that "not-knowing" is repeated and elaborated in the transference without ever becoming a literal site to which I might return.

Through the transference, psychoanalysis nevertheless charts primary relational dispositions and scenes, articulating the scenes of address in which selves variably emerge. Although Laplanche's perspective is not fully compatible with object-relations theorists such as Christopher Bollas, we can see in both approaches a certain attentiveness to what Bollas has called the "unthought known."[12] Bollas was instrumental in introducing the concept of the analyst as a "transformational object"; he suggested that clinicians should return to Freud's self-analysis and consider more attentively the uses of the counter-transference within psychoanalytic work. In *The Shadow of the Object: Psychoanalysis of the Unthought Known*, Bollas describes being "re-cruited" into the environment of the analysand, tacitly positioned and "used" by the analysand as an "object" who belongs to an earlier scene. The counter-transference responds to what is not fully known by the analysand:

> The analyst is invited to fulfill differing and changing object representations in the environment, but such observations on our part are the rare moments of clarity in the countertransference. For a very long period of time, and perhaps it never ends, we are being taken into the patient's environmental idiom, and for considerable stretches of time we do not know who we are, what function we are meant to fulfill, or our fate as his object. (202)

Following Winnicott, Bollas makes the case that the analyst must not only allow himself to become used but even "be prepared on occasion to become situationally ill" (204). The analyst allows himself to be deployed in the environmental idiom of the analysand at the same time as he develops a reflective and deliberate capacity for analysis within that difficult situation. Bollas discusses several clinical examples, in which he shows the "expressive uses" of the counter-transference within analytic work. One patient speaks and then falls silent, leaving Bollas with a sense of aloneness and disorientation. When he finally gives voice to this sense within the session, it is to suggest that for and with him the patient has effectively recreated the environment in which she had felt suddenly isolated and lost as a young child. He asks whether she has asked him to inhabit this experience through her long pauses so that he can know what it was she then felt. What she offers, then, is less a narrative than a recreated scene of suddenly abandoned communication and a disorienting loss of contact. There is a narrative dimension to his subsequent intervention since he asks whether this experience belongs to her past. The point, however, is less to reconstruct the precise details of the story than to establish another possibility for communication within the transference. When he suggests that she has given him the position of re-experiencing her own experience of loss and absence, he communicates to her in a way that has not been done before, and the conversation that follows, explicitly thematizing this broken form of communication, constitutes a more connected mode of communication, working to alter the default scene of address.

The model of psychoanalytic intervention that Bollas affirms constitutes a significant departure from the classical notion of the cold and distant analyst who keeps every counter-transferential issue to himself. For Bollas, "the analyst will need to become lost in the patient's world, lost in the sense of not knowing what his feelings and states of mind are in any one moment" (253). Later he remarks that only when the analyst presents himself to be used by the patient is there any hope that the counter-transference can facilitate a new set of object relations: "Only by making a good object (the analyst) go somewhat mad can such a patient believe in his analysis and *know that the analyst has been where he has been and has survived and emerged intact*" (254).

Bollas clearly suggests that the analyst must allow him- or herself to be impinged upon by the client, even undergo a kind of dispossession of self, as well as to maintain a reflective psychoanalytic distance and attitude. In describing Winnicott's way of introducing his own thoughts into the analytic session, Bollas writes:

> they were for him subjective objects, and he put them to the patient as objects between patient and analyst rather than as official psychoanalytic decodings of the person's unconscious life. The effect of his attitude is crucial, as his interpretations were meant to be played with—kicked around, mulled over, torn to pieces—rather than regarded as the official version of the truth. (206)

The aim here appears to be to facilitate what Bollas describes as the "articulation of heretofore inarticulate elements of psychic life, or what I term the unthought known." "Articulation" is a broad category for describing various modes of expression and communication, some of them narrative and some not. Although here Bollas does not consider the limits of articulability, that is, the unthought that can never quite be "known," such a consideration would seem to constitute a necessary counterpart to his explorations. Indeed, primary forms of impingement that cannot be fully or clearly articulated within the analytic process are doubtless at work in the scene of address. Full articulability should not be deemed the final goal of psychoanalytic work in any event, for that goal would imply a linguistic and egoic mastery over unconscious material that would seek to transform the unconscious itself into reflective, conscious articulation—an impossible ideal, and one that undercuts one of the most important tenets of psychoanalysis. The "I" cannot knowingly fully recover what impels it, since its formation remains prior to its elaboration as reflexive self-knowing. This reminds us that conscious experience is only one dimension of psychic life, and that we cannot achieve by consciousness or language a full mastery over those primary relations of dependency and impressionability that form and constitute us in persistent and obscure ways.

The ways that an infant has been handled or addressed can be gleaned only indirectly from the social environment that the analysand later orchestrates. Although there is always a specificity to that environment, one can make the general claim that primary impressions are not just *received* by an ego, but are formative of it. The ego does not come into being without a prior encounter, a primary relation, a set of inaugural impressions from elsewhere. When Winnicott describes the ego as a relational process, he is disputing the view that the ego is constituted and there from the outset of life. He is also positing the primacy of relationality to any bounded sense of self. If the ego, as Bollas and Lacan would agree, "long precedes the arrival of the subject,"[13] that means only that the relational process that seeks to negotiate a differentiation from the unconscious and from the other is not yet articulated in speech, not yet capable of reflective self-deliberation. In any case, the ego is not an entity or a substance, but an array of relations and processes, implicated in the world of primary caregivers in ways that constitute its very definition.

Moreover, if in the inaugural moments of the "I" I am implicated by the other's address and demand, then there is some convergence between the ethical scene in which my life is, from the start, bound up with others and the psychoanalytic scene that establishes the intersubjective conditions of my own emergence, individuation, and survivability. Insofar as it recapitulates and reenacts in refracted form the primary scenes of address, the transference operates in the service of narrating a life, assisting in the building of a life story. Working in tandem with the counter-transference, the transference interrupts the suspect coherence that narrative forms sometimes construct, a coherence that can displace from consideration the rhetorical features of the scene of address, which both draw me back to the scene of not knowing, of being overwhelmed, and also, in the present, sustain me.

At its best, the transference provides what Winnicott terms a holding environment and offers a bodily presence in a temporal present that provides the conditions for a sustaining address.[14] This is not to say that transference does not contribute to the narrating of a life: one may be able to tell one's story better when being "held" in the Winnicottian sense. But there are expressive dimensions of that "holding" that cannot be described through narrative means. There is no reason to call into question the importance of narrating a life, in its partiality and provisionality. I am sure that transference can facilitate narration and that narrating a life has a crucial function, especially for those whose involuntary experience of discontinuity afflicts them in profound ways. No one can live in a radically non-narratable world or survive a radically non-narratable life. But it is still necessary to remember that what qualifies as an "articulation" and "expression" of psychic material exceeds narration, and that articulations of all kinds have their necessary limits, given the structuring effects of what remains persistently inarticulable.

Sometimes a narrative voice can remain, for instance, shorn of its narrative powers. In Kafka's story, after Georg appears to throw himself off the bridge and end his life, there is still a narrative voice that uncannily remains, reporting on the noises that populate that event's aftermath. The final line of the text, "at this moment an unending stream of traffic was just going over the bridge," is spoken by some voice that claims to be present to the moment described, and the third-person perspective is disjoined from the character of Georg, who has already let himself drop below. It is as if character is vanquished, but voice remains. Although Georg is gone, some narrative voice survives to remark upon the scene. It may be the voice of the imaginary friend to whom both Georg and his father were said to have written, and it may be that this friend turns out to have been writing the two of them, transitively, all along. The final line, referring to the "traffic" going over the bridge, makes use of the German word *Verkehr*, a term used for sexual intercourse, as well. The ambiguity suggests that this death is also a pleasure, perhaps an ecstatic relinquishing of discrete bodily boundary.[15] The voice that emerges to report this fact, a voice that belongs to no one and whose proximity to the event is logically impossible, is purely fictive, perhaps the sublimity of fiction itself. Although the story narrates a death, it also preserves a voice in the final narrative line, suggesting that a human something survives, that narration has some propitious relation to survival. What remains peculiar, however, is that this is a written voice with no body and no name, a voice extracted from the scene of address itself, one whose extraction, paradoxically, forms the basis of its survival. The voice is ghostly, impossible, disembodied, and yet it persists, living on.

In a well-known letter written to Benjamin on December 17, 1934, Adorno reviews Benjamin's essay on Kafka and considers the conditions for survival that Kafka's texts provide. He begins by noting that he is not "in the slightest position to pass 'judgment' upon [Benjamin's] essay," knowingly referencing the potentially fatal problems associated with judgment of this kind. Adorno's remarks to Benjamin are the usual ones: Benjamin gives an account of an "archaic" and primal history that is irrecoverable, whereas Adorno insists that the loss of a concept of our "historical age" is a dialectical loss, one that has to be understood as a loss *for us*, under these specific historical conditions.

Adorno moves to a consideration of guilt and fatality via the figure of Odradek, a thinglike creature, fundamentally nonconceptualizable, described in Kafka's parable "Cares of a Family Man."[16] Odradek, whose name admits of no clear etymology, is another son-like figure who vacates his human form in the face of parental judgment. Odradek appears to be at once a spool of thread and an odd star who is able to balance himself on one of his points. His laughter is the kind "that has no lungs behind it. It sounds rather like the rustling of fallen leaves" (428). Barely anything of the human form survives in his survival, and the narrator of the story, a paternal voice, seriously doubts whether Odradek is even a remnant of a creature with "intelligible shape." Neither Adorno nor Benjamin takes the psychoanalytic route in explaining this de-humanized form. But Adorno understands that vacating the human form in some ways promises the overcoming of a fatal guilt. He writes:

> If [Odradek's] origin lies with the father of the house, does he not then precisely represent the anxious *concern* and danger for the latter, does he not anticipate precisely the overcoming of the creaturely state of guilt, and is not this concern—truly a case of Heidegger put right side up—the secret key, indeed, the most indubitable promise of *hope*, precisely through the overcoming of the house itself? Certainly, as the other face of the world of things, Odradek is a sign of distortion—but precisely as such he is also a

motif of transcendence, namely, of the ultimate limit and of the reconciliation of the organic and inorganic, or of the overcoming of death: Odradek "lives on." (69)

Odradek "lives on" in much the same way the formless final voice "lives on" at the end of "The Judgment."[17] In this sense, for Adorno the movement by which human form is vacated is the means by which something like hope arrives, as if suspending the social parameters of the subject—"overcoming the house"—were what is required for survival. Since Adorno refuses to see this survival as an eternal or archaic transcendence, he must argue that certain conditions establish distortion or disfiguration as the sign of hope or survival. In his "Notes on Kafka" Adorno writes, "the social origin of the individual ultimately reveals itself as the power to annihilate him. Kafka's work is an attempt to absorb this."[18] This seems to be a truth about modernity or, indeed, a truth that marks modernity as such. As a corollary to this claim, the attempt to vacate the social (in its current form) seems to promise the hope of survival.

The narrative voice reports on his direct address to Odradek: "Well, what's your name?" "Odradek," he says. "And where do you live?" "No fixed abode." There is a question, "Who are you?" and then, as a reply, a voice again, but no human form. The narrator indirectly humanizes Odradek through the third-person pronoun as well as through direct address. The paternal voice does not exactly despise him, since the parable ends with the line: "He does no harm to anyone that I can see; but the idea that he is likely to survive me I find almost painful." It is almost painful, but not quite. And in that "not quite" we can see some hope for Odradek's survival that outlives a near total dehumanization.

The social origins of the individual, even within modernity, constitute one way for survival to be threatened. Annihilation threatens from the other side as well when the very transcendence of the social threatens to undermine the social conditions of life itself. After all, no one survives without being addressed; no one survives to tell his or her story without first being inaugurated into language by being called upon, offered some stories, brought into the discursive world of the story. Only later can one then find one's way in language, only after it has been imposed, only after it has produced a web of relations in which affectivity achieves articulation in some form. One enters into a communicative environment as an infant and child who is addressed and who learns certain ways of addressing in return. The default patterns of this relationality emerge as the opacity within any account of oneself.

I would suggest that the structure of address is not a feature of narrative, one of its many and variable attributes, but an interruption of narrative. The moment the story is addressed to someone, it assumes a rhetorical dimension that is not reducible to a narrative function. It presumes that someone, and it seeks to recruit and act upon that someone. Something is being done with language when the account that I give begins: it is invariably interlocutory, ghosted, laden, persuasive, and tactical. It may well seek to communicate a truth, but it can do this, if it can, only by exercising a relational dimension of language.

This view has implications for the making of moral judgments as well: namely, that the structure of address conditions the making of judgments about someone or his or her actions; that it is not reducible to the judgment; and that the judgment, unbeholden to the ethics implied by the structure of address, tends toward violence.

But here, for the time being, I am concerned with a suspect coherence that sometimes attaches to narrative, specifically, with the way in which narrative coherence may foreclose an ethical resource—namely, an acceptance of the limits of knowability in oneself and others. To hold a person accountable for his or her life in narrative form may even be to require a falsification of that life in order to satisfy the criterion of a certain kind of ethics, one that tends to break with relationality. One could perhaps satisfy the burden of proof that another imposes upon an account, but what sort of inter-locutory scene would be produced in consequence? The relation be-tween the interlocutors is established as one between a judge who reviews evidence and a supplicant trying to measure up to an in-decipherable burden of proof. We are then not that far from Kafka. Indeed, if we require that someone be able to tell in story form the reasons why his or her life has taken the path it has, that is, to be a coherent autobiographer, we may be preferring the seamlessness of the story to something we might tentatively call the truth of the person, a truth that, to a certain degree, for reasons we have already suggested, might well become more clear in moments of interruption, stoppage, open-endedness—in enigmatic articulations that cannot easily be translated into narrative form.

This brings us closer to an understanding of transference as a practice of ethics. Indeed, if, in the name of ethics, we (violently) require that another do a certain violence to herself, and do it in front of us by offering a narrative account or issuing a confession, then, conversely, if we permit, sustain, and accommodate the inter-ruption, a certain practice of nonviolence may follow. If violence is the act by which a subject seeks to reinstall its mastery and unity, then nonviolence may well follow from living the persistent challenge to egoic mastery that our obligations to others induce and require.

This failure to narrate fully may well indicate the way in which we are, from the start, ethically implicated in the lives of others. Although some would say that to be a split subject, or a subject whose access to itself is forever opaque, incapable of self-grounding, is precisely *not* to have the grounds for agency and the conditions for accountability, the way in which we are, from the start, interrupted by alterity may render us incapable of offering narrative closure for our lives. The purpose here is not to celebrate a certain notion of incoherence, but only to point out that our "incoherence" establishes the way in which we are constituted in relationality: implicated, be-holden, derived, sustained by a social world that is beyond us and before us.

To say, as some do, that the self *must* be narrated, that only the narrated self can be intelligible and survive, is to say that we cannot survive with an unconscious. It is to say, in effect, that the unconscious threatens us with an insupportable unintelligibility, and for that reason we must oppose it. The "I" who makes such an utterance will surely, in one form or another, be besieged by what it disavows. An "I" who takes this stand—and it is *a stand*, it must be a stand, an upright, wakeful, knowing stand—believes that it survives without the unconscious. Or, if it accepts an unconscious, this "I" accepts it as something that is thoroughly recuperable by the knowing "I," perhaps as a possession, in the belief that the unconscious can be fully and exhaustively translated into what is conscious. It is easy to see that this is a defended stance, but it remains to be seen in what this particular defense consists. It is, after all, the stand that many make against psychoanalysis itself. In the language that articulates opposition to a non-narrativizable beginning resides the fear that the absence of narrative will spell a certain threat, a threat to life, and will pose the risk, if not the certainty, of a certain kind of death, the death of a subject who cannot, who can never, fully recuperate the conditions of its own emergence.

But this death, if it is a death, is only the death of a certain kind of subject, one that was never possible to begin with, the death of a fantasy of impossible mastery, and so a loss of what one never had. In other words, it is a necessary grief.

The "I" and the "You"

> I am you,
> > If I am
>
> > > —Paul Celan

So, I try to begin a story about myself, and I begin somewhere, marking a time, trying to begin a sequence, offering, perhaps, causal links or at least narrative structure. I narrate, and I bind myself as I narrate, give an account of myself, offer an account to an other in the form of a story that might well work to summarize how and why I am.

But my effort at self-summarization fails, and fails necessarily, when the "I" who is introduced in the opening line as a narrative voice cannot give an account of how it became an "I" who might narrate itself or this story in particular. And as I make a sequence and link one event with another, offering motivations to illuminate the bridge, making patterns clear, identifying certain events or moments of recognition as pivotal, even marking certain recurring patterns as fundamental, I do not merely communicate something about my past, though that is doubtless part of what I do. I also enact the self I am trying to describe; the narrative "I" is reconstituted at every moment it is invoked in the narrative itself. That invocation is, paradoxically, a performative and non-narrative act, even as it functions as the fulcrum for narrative itself. I am, in other words, doing something with that "I"—elaborating and positioning it in relation to a real or imagined audience—which is something other than telling a story about it, even though "telling" remains part of what I do. Which part of "telling" is an acting upon the other, a production of the "I" anew?

Just as there is a performative and allocutory action that this "I" performs, there is a limit to what the "I" can actually recount. This "I" is spoken and articulated, and though it seems to ground the narrative I tell, it is the most ungrounded moment in the narrative. The one story that the "I" cannot tell is the story of its own emergence as an "I" who not only speaks but comes to give an account of itself. In this sense, a story is being told, but the "I" who tells the story, who may well appear within the story as the first-person narrator, constitutes a point of opacity and interrupts a sequence, induces a break or eruption of the non-narrativizable in the midst of the story. So the story of myself that I tell, foregrounding the "I" who I am and inserting it into the relevant sequences of something called my life, fails to give an account of myself at the moment that I am introduced. Indeed, I am introduced as one for whom no account can or will be given. I am giving an account of myself, but there is no account to be given when it comes to the formation of this speaking "I" who would narrate its life. The more I narrate, the less accountable I prove to be. The "I" ruins its own story, contrary to its best intentions.

The "I" cannot give a final or adequate account of itself because it cannot return to the scene of address by which it is inaugurated and it cannot narrate all of the rhetorical dimensions of the structure of address in which the account itself takes place. These rhetorical dimensions of the scene of address cannot be reduced to narrative. This becomes clear in the context of a transference or, rather, in the model of communication that transference provides, for there one is spoken to, on occasion, and one also speaks, and always, indirectly or directly, in the form of an address.

If I am trying to give an account of myself, it is always *to* someone, to one whom I presume to receive my words in some way, although I do not and cannot know always in what way. In fact, the one who is positioned as the receiver may not be receiving at all, may be engaged in something that cannot under any circumstances be called "receiving," doing nothing more for me than establishing a certain site, a position, a structural place where the relation to a possible reception is articulated. So whether or not there is an other who actually receives is beside the point, since the point will be that there is a site where the relation to a possible reception takes form. The forms this relation to a possible reception can take are many: no one can hear this; this one will surely understand this; I will be refused here, misunderstood there, judged, dismissed, accepted, or embraced. Here as elsewhere, the transference brings forth a scenario from the past, enacting precisely what cannot be given in another expressive form, at the same time that a new and possibly altered relation is wrought from this more archaic resource. To be more precise, the transference is living proof that the past is not past, since the form that the past now takes is in the present orchestration of the relation to the other that is the transference itself. In this sense, for the past to be lived in the present, narration is not the only route, and not necessarily the most affectively engaging: the past is there and now, structuring and animating the very contours of a default relationality, animating the transference, the recruitment and use of the analyst, orchestrating the scene of address.

One goes to analysis, I presume, to have someone receive one's words. This produces a quandary, since the one who might receive the words is unknown in large part; one who receives becomes, in a certain way, an allegory for reception itself, for the phantasmatic relation to receiving that is articulated to, or at least in the presence of, an other. But if this is an allegory, it is not reducible to a structure of reception that would apply equally well to everyone, although it might give us the general structures within which a particular life could be understood. Subjects who narrate ourselves in the first person encounter a common predicament. There are clearly times when I cannot tell the story in a straight line, and I lose my thread, and I start again, and I forgot something crucial, and it is too hard to think about how to weave it in. I start thinking, thinking, there must be some conceptual thread that will provide a narrative here, some lost link, some possibility for chronology, and the "I" becomes increasingly conceptual, increasingly awake, focused, determined. At this point, when I near the prospect of intellectual self-sufficiency in the presence of the other, nearly excluding him or her from my horizon, the thread of my story unravels. If I achieve that self-sufficiency, my relation to the other is lost. I then relive an abandonment and dependency that is overwhelming. Something other than a purely conceptual elaboration of experience emerges at such a juncture. The "I" who narrates finds that it cannot direct its narration, finds that it can give an account neither of its inability to narrate nor of why narration breaks down. It comes to experience itself or, rather, re-experience itself as radically, if not irretrievably, unknowing about who it is. Then the "I" is no longer imparting a narrative to a receiving analyst or other; the "I" is staging a scene, recruiting the other into the scene of its own opacity to itself. The "I" is breaking down in certain very specific ways in front of the other or, to anticipate Levinas, in the face of the Other (originally I wrote, "the in face of the Other," indicating that my syntax was already breaking down) or, indeed, by virtue of the Other's face, voice, or silent presence. The "I" finds that, in the presence of an other, it is breaking down. It does not know itself; perhaps it never will. But is that the task, to know oneself? Is the final aim to achieve an adequate narrative account of a life? And should it be? Is the task to cover over through a narrative means the breakage, the rupture, that is constitutive of the "I," which quite forcefully binds the elements together as if it were perfectly possible, as if the break could be mended and defensive mastery restored?

Before the other one cannot give an account of the "I" who has been trying all along to give an account of itself. A certain humility must emerge in this process, perhaps also a certain knowingness about the limits of what there is to know. Perhaps every analysand becomes, in this sense, a lay Kantian. But there is something more: a point about language and its historicity. *The means by which subject constitution occurs is not the same as the narrative form the reconstruction of that constitution attempts to provide.* So what is the role of language in constituting the subject? And what different role does it assume when it seeks to recuperate or reconstitute the conditions of its own constitution? First, there is the question "How is it that my constitution became 'my own'?" Where and when does this presumption of property and belonging take place? We cannot tell a story about this, but perhaps there is some other way in which it is available to us, even available to us through language. In the moment in which I say "I," I am not only citing the pronominal place of the "I" in language, but at once attesting to and taking distance from a primary impingement, a primary way in which I am, prior to acquiring an "I," a being who has been touched, moved, fed, changed, put to sleep, established as the subject and object of speech. My infantile body has not only been touched, moved, and arranged, but those impingements operated as "tactile signs" that registered in my formation. These signs communicate to me in ways that are not reducible to vocalization. They are signs of an other, but they are also the traces from which an "I" will eventually emerge, an "I" who will never be able, fully, to recover or read these signs, for whom these signs will remain in part overwhelming and unreadable, enigmatic and formative.

Earlier we considered the difference between a concept such as "articulation" in Bollas's work and that of narration, suggesting that what is "expressive" and "articulated" may not always take narrative form in order to constitute a psychic transformation of some kind or to provide a positive alteration in a transferential relation. At that time, I proposed, not only that a term like *articulation* suggests the limits to narrative accountability as a desired model for expression, but that articulation itself has its necessary limits and that full articulation would be as problematic an aspiration for psychoanalysis as narrative closure and mastery. Jean Laplanche contends that the limit to full articulation arrives, not because of a Lacanian "bar" that forecloses the return to a primary *jouissance*, but because of the overwhelming and enigmatic impressions made by the adult world in its specificity on the child. For Laplanche, there is no Other in some symbolic sense, just the various others who constitute the caregiving adults in a child's world. Indeed, for Laplanche there is no reason to assume that these caregivers must be oedipally organized as "father" and "mother."[19]

Whereas for Bollas the environment into which the analyst is recruited through the transference and counter-transference is one in which the analysand engages in an unknowing yet active orchestration of the scene and "use" of the analyst, for Laplanche it would seem that the primary experience for the infant is invariably that of being overwhelmed, not only "helpless" by virtue of undeveloped motor capacities, but profoundly clueless about the impingements of the adult world. What emerges as enigmatic within the transference, then, is a residue of a primary situation of being overwhelmed that precedes the formation of the unconscious and of the drives.

Laplanche writes of the "perceptive and motor opening to the world" that characterizes the primary condition of infantile life, working in the service of self-preservation. The infant must be open to the environment to adapt to its terms and secure the satisfaction of its most basic needs. This openness also constitutes a precocious exposure to the adult world of unconscious sexuality, though he is clear that sexuality is not derived from self-preservation. It emerges as a consequence of a social world, of messages or signifiers that are imposed upon the child from this environment and produce over-whelming and unmasterable primary impressions for which no ready adaptation is possible. Indeed, these primary impressions constitute a primary trauma that is unsustainable, what he calls "absolute primary process." Consequently, a primary repression takes place (no agency effects this repression, there is only the agency of repression itself) that institutes the unconscious and establishes the "first object-sources, that is, the sources of the drives."[20] What is repressed is a "thing-representation" of these primary impressions: as a consequence of trauma, an originally external object becomes installed as a source or cause of sexual drives. Drives (life drives and death drives) are not considered primary—they follow from an interioriza-tion of the enigmatic desires of others and carry the residue of those originally external desires. As a result, every drive is beset by a for-eignness (*étrangèreté*), and the "I" finds itself to be foreign to itself in its most elemental impulses.

Laplanche is aware that this account disputes both the primacy of drives and the attribution of their source in a pure biology: "as for the relation of the drive to the body and to erogenous zones, this relation should not be conceived with the body as starting-point, but rather as the action of repressed object-sources on the body" (191). In effect, the infant cannot handle what Laplanche calls the "messages" from the adult world. It represses them in the form of "thing-representations" (a concept that Freud offers in his theorizations of the unconscious), which later emerge in enigmatic form for the partially knowing subject of desire. This irrecoverable and nonthematic origin of affect cannot be recovered through proper articulation, whether in narrative form or in any other medium of expression. We can, meta-theoretically, reconstruct the scenario of primary repression, but no subject can narrate the story of a primary repression that constitutes the irrecoverable basis of his or her own formation.

For Laplanche, primary repression reconstitutes overwhelming affect as "thing-representations" in an unconscious, and these emerge in turn as "enigmatic signifiers." This process is the consequence of the adult world, understood as "entirely infiltrated with unconscious and sexual significations," imposing itself upon the infant, who "possesses neither the emotional nor physiological responses which correspond to the sexualized messages that are proposed to it" (188). Similarly, Laplanche remarks that the infant's question is not whether he or she may have the breast (a question that presupposes a prior exposure to an incestuous prohibition), but "What does the breast want of me?" (188). Desire emerges first from the outside and in overwhelming form, and it retains this exterior and foreign quality once it becomes the subject's own desire. Thus, if there is a question that emerges within the transference that one might derive from a Laplanchian approach to infantile sexuality and the primary conditions for the formation of the subject, it would not be "Who are you?" but "Who is this 'you' who demands something of me I cannot give?" He remarks in an interview with Cathy Caruth that

> It's a very big error on the part of psychoanalysts to try to make a theory of knowledge starting from so-called psychoanalysis—for instance, starting from the breast and the reality of the breast. Or

even Winnicott's starting from the first not-me possession, and building the external world beginning with what he called the transitional object, and so on. The problem, on our human level, is that the other does not have to be reconstructed. The other is prior to the subject. The other on the sexual level is intruding the biological world. So you don't have to construct it, it first comes to you, as an enigma.[21]

Laplanche claims that at first the infant passively registers these enigmatic signifiers. Repression constitutes a first occurrence of an action, but it is a deed, we might say, that precedes any doer. These enigmatic signifiers, once repressed, proceed to "attack" from the inside, and there is something of this enigmatic attack that survives in the adult experience of sexuality as well. There is something at work in and on one's desire that is not recoverable through thematization or narrative. The aim of one's own impulses not only becomes enigmatic and inscrutable to the child, but remains to a certain extent that way throughout life. This situation gives rise to the child's theorization, the attempt to link these attacks, to give some coherence to them.

Indeed, Laplanche suggests that theory itself emerges from this predicament as a way to establish patterns and meanings for an enigma that constitutes our fundamental opacity to ourselves. In a psychoanalytic transference, one can neither recover nor eliminate this enigma (that would be to recover and eliminate primary process itself).[22] For Laplanche, the transference reproduces and renews the primal seduction scene. The question is thus not who the analyst represents but only "What does the analyst want of me?" Thus Laplanche, in the interview with Caruth, makes his difference from Winnicott clear: "instead of saying the first not-me possession, the problem for the human sexual being is to have a first-me possession. That is, to build an ego starting from too much otherness." We do not move from an ego that must reconstruct an object world, but we find ourselves besieged from the start by an enigmatic alterity that makes the elaboration of an "I" a persistently difficult achievement. The task is not to move from an established ego to a world of others, to move beyond narcissism to the possibility of attachment. Rather, attachment is already overdetermined from the start, since the other besieges and engulfs the infant, and the emergence from this primary impingement is a struggle that can have only limited success.

Laplanche thus posits a foreign desire as a precondition of "one's own" desire. Who desires when "I" desire? There seems to be another at work in my desire, and this *étrangèreté* disrupts any effort to make sense of myself as a bounded and separate being. I may try to tell the story of myself, but another story is already at work in me, and there is no way to distinguish between the "I" who has emerged from this infantile condition and the "you"—the set of "you's"— who inhabits and dispossesses my desire from the outset. We might consider, then, that the failure of Georg to fully extricate himself from his parents, the "too much" attachment that leads to his suicidal conclusion, can be read in a Laplanchian vein. Was the death sentence his father's act or his own, and was there any way to disjoin the two actions from one another? Why does the father collapse on the bed after he has sentenced his son to death? And is that son forced from the room by the strength of the condemnation, or is he moved down the steps and toward the water through an agency of his own? *Es triebt ihn*—what is this "it," this foreignness, that motivates the son toward his acrobatic death? If the parents cannot be extricated from the son's desire, then it would appear that the "agency" of desire is less grounded in the separate self of the son than in a foreign object lodged there, animating him in nontransparent ways. Perhaps some separation might have saved him, or perhaps death itself was the longing for an ultimate separation from his parents fatally twinned with his undying love for them.

The priority of the other for Laplanche leads him to certain ethical conclusions. He remarks in his interview with Caruth that our first questions about death are not about our own but, rather, about the death of others: "Why must the other die?" "Why did the other die?" The other, we might say, comes first, and this means that there is no reference to one's own death that is not at once a reference to the death of the other. In the introduction to *Life and Death in Psychoanalysis,* he writes (and Caruth quotes): "If a certain ethic in relation to death might be evolved from the Freudian attitude, it would be in the sense of a distrust concerning every form of enthusiasm, and of a lucidity that does not hide the irreducible meshing of my death with that of the other."[23]

This last remark suggests that the psychoanalytic approach to the primacy of the Other implies an ethical caution against enthusiasms that might make one impervious to the precariousness of life. It also counsels that one cannot preserve one's own death at the expense of the other without the other's death implicating me in my own. There is, as it were, a sociality at the basis of the "I" and its finitude from which one cannot—and ought not to—escape.

In "Responsibility and Response," Laplanche considers Freud's reflections on the relation between responsibility and psychoanalysis, focusing on the curious question of whether one must take responsibility for one's dreams.[24] Do dreams reflect only one's own mind or do they register the thoughts and desires of others? If the thoughts and desires of others have entered my dream, then I am, even at an unconscious level, beset by the other. This leads Laplanche, following Freud, to focus on the "humiliation" that psychoanalysis entails for the conception of the human being, one that Laplanche associates with a Copernican revolution within the sphere of psychology. He writes that "man is not at home with himself in himself [*chez lui en lui*], which means that in himself, he is not the master and that finally (here, these are my terms), he is decentered" (156). This decentering follows from the way in which others, from the outset, transmit certain messages to us, instilling their thoughts in our own, producing an indistinguishability between the other and myself at the heart of who I am.

This consideration of a Copernican revolution in the conception of the human being leads Laplanche to a brief discussion of Levinas. There he writes that Levinas's early work on Husserl interested him, but that what follows could not be said to have influenced him (162). He states his major difference with Levinas: "the Copernican decentering holds not only for the autocentric perceptive subject and for the cogito, but also for the subject who is considered autocentric in time; centered in his adult being" (163). He believes that Levinas, like Heidegger, failed to decenter adult experience or, rather, failed to see that adult experience is decentered by infantile experience all along: "If one seeks to take this seriously, according to Freud, the primacy of infancy decenters us as irremediably—and as without reflexivity—as the unconscious or the id" (163). The primary question toward the other that emerges from the perspective of infancy is: "Who is this person who speaks to me? [*Quelle est la personne qui me parle?*]" (163). The other who speaks to me is not in a "reciprocal" exchange or balanced communication. The situation is, from the start, asymmetrical, and the "I" finds itself disarmed and passive in its relation to the message from the other. Under these conditions, the infant can make only an inadequate translation and response.

What, then, is the relation between the first response as Laplanche describes it and responsibility? He turns to the story of Job and makes use of a Levinasian language to describe the travail of response under a situation of absolute dissymmetry. The infant responds as Job responds to a seemingly cruel God, that is, to an "unnameable persecution" (166). This persecutory impression becomes a sexualized capacity for sadism, one to which our dreams testify, Laplanche claims, and which is made manifest in cruelty and war. Levinas would surely not follow Laplanche on this last turn. Laplanche, however, points out that the response of the child to the overwhelming adult can be to recenter himself, or to seek recentering as a way of life. This (Ptolemaic) task would seek to deny the unconscious, recenter the subject, and so make the adult in question more vulnerable to acting out sadistic impulses that it refuses to understand as its own constitutive potential. The transference can be the place where this scene can be re-elaborated. But there is no getting rid of this unconscious, no full substitution of the ego for the id, and surely no recentering of the subject without unleashing unacceptable sadism and cruelty. To remain decentered, interestingly, means to remain implicated in the death of the other and so at a distance from the unbridled cruelty (the limit case of uncritical enthusiasm) in which the self seeks to separate from its constitutive sociality and annihilate the other.

The infant enters the world given over from the start to a language and to a series of signs, broadly construed, that begin to structure an already operative mode of receptivity and demand. From this primary experience of *having been given over from the start*, an "I" subsequently emerges. And the "I," regardless of its claims to mastery, will never get over having been given over from the start in this way. Levinas might be said to indicate something similar. He speaks of a passivity prior to passivity, and there he means to indicate the difference between a subject who undergoes passivity, who relates to that passivity through a certain act of reflexivity, and a passivity that is prior to the subject, the condition of its own subjectivation, its primary impressionability.

Here the other is, as it were, the condition of possibility of my affective life, installed within me as an object-source that gives rise to the drives and desires that are mine. From within the object-relations perspective, the primary impressions constitute objects, exterior but proximate, to which an emergent self might attach itself to satisfy basic needs. It follows from this view that the infant will be disposed to love any and every thing which emerges as an "object" (rather than not love at all, fail to attach, and jeopardize its survival). This is a scandal, of course, since it shows us that love, from the outset, is without judgment, and that, to a certain extent, it remains without judgment or, at least, without good judgment for the rest of its career.

What I am trying to describe is the condition of the subject, but it is not *mine*: I do not own it. It is prior to what constitutes the sphere of what might be owned or claimed by me. It persistently undoes the claim of "mineness," mocks it, sometimes gently, sometimes violently. It is a way of being constituted by an Other that precedes the formation of the sphere of the *mine* itself. Primary impressionability is not a feature or predicate of an established self so that I might say, by way of a warning, "I am impressionable." I could say that, but it would be a paradoxical form of speaking, and I would not be referencing impressionability in its primary form. I come up with such statements as an attempt to come to terms with what remains enigmatic, and so my statements and theories are prompted by the very impressions and drives that they seek to explain. At this level, we are not yet referring to boundaries in the process of formation, we are not yet seeking recourse to a capacity for reflexivity, for self-reference, the linguistic support for self-possession. This is a domain in which the grammar of the subject cannot hold, for dispossession in and through another is prior to becoming an "I" who might claim, on occasion, and always with some irony, to possess itself.

You may think that I am in fact telling a story about the prehistory of the subject, one that I have been arguing cannot be told. There are two responses to this objection. (1) That there is no final or adequate narrative reconstruction of the prehistory of the speaking "I" does not mean we cannot narrate it; it only means that at the moment when we narrate we become speculative philosophers or fiction writers. (2) This prehistory has never stopped happening and, as such, is not a prehistory in any chronological sense. It is not done with, over, relegated to a past, which then becomes part of a causal or narrative reconstruction of the self. On the contrary, that prehistory interrupts the story I have to give of myself, makes every account of myself partial and failed, and constitutes, in a way, my failure to be fully accountable for my actions, my final "irresponsibility," one for which I may be forgiven only because I could not do otherwise. This not being able to do otherwise is our common predicament.

That prehistory continues to happen every time I enunciate myself. In speaking the "I," I undergo something of what cannot be captured or assimilated by the "I," since I always arrive too late to myself. (Nietzsche's bees in *The Genealogy of Morals* clearly prefigure the psychoanalytic concept of *Nachträglichkeit*.) I can never provide the account of myself that both certain forms of morality and some models of mental health require, namely, that the self deliver itself in coherent narrative form. The "I" is the moment of failure in every narrative effort to give an account of oneself. It remains the unaccounted for and, in that sense, constitutes the failure that the very project of self-narration requires. Every effort to give an account of oneself is bound to encounter this failure, and to founder upon it.

But perhaps there is no necessary reason why this encounter with failure should take place. After all, it is important to remember the stand against the unconscious, the one that claims, after all, that a non-narrativizable self cannot survive and is not viable. For such a stand, it seems, the very livability of the subject resides in its narrativizability. The postulation of the non-narrativizable poses a threat to such a subject, indeed, can pose the threat of death. I don't think it inevitably takes the generalized form: If I cannot tell a story about myself, then I will die. But it can take this form under situations of moral duress: If I am not able to give an account of some of my actions, then I would rather die, because I cannot find myself as the author of these actions, and I cannot explain myself to those my actions may have hurt. Surely, there is a certain desperation there, where I repeat myself and where my repetitions enact again and again the site of my radical unself-knowingness. How am I to live under these circumstances? Perhaps death would be better than to continue to live with this inability to render myself ethical through an account that not only explains what I do but allows me to assume greater agency in deciding what to do.

What is striking about such extremes of self-beratement is the grandiose notion of the transparent "I" that is presupposed as the ethical ideal. This is hardly a belief in which self-acceptance (a humility about one's constitutive limitations) or generosity (a disposition toward the limits of others) might find room to flourish. Surely there are moments of repetition and opacity and anguish, which usually compel a journey to the analyst, or if not to the analyst, to someone—an addressee—who might receive the story and, in receiving, alter it some. The other represents the prospect that the story might be given back in new form, that fragments might be linked in some way, that some part of opacity might be brought to light. The other witnesses and registers what cannot be narrated, functioning as one who might discern a narrative thread, though mainly as one whose practice of listening enacts a receptive relation to the self that the self, in its dire straits of self-beratement, cannot offer itself. And it seems crucial to recognize, not only that the anguish and opacity of the "I" is witnessed by the other, but that the other can become the name for one's anguish and opacity: "*You* are my anguish, surely. *You* are opaque: who are you? Who is this you that resides in me, from whom I cannot extricate myself?" The other can also refuse, disrupt, or "surprise" this identification, separating off the phantasm that lodges under the other's name and offering it as an object for analysis within the interlocutory scene.

Who speaks in this address, the address of the transference? What speaks here? Where is the "here" and when is the "now" of transferential time? If that which I am defies narrative capture, compels speculation, insists itself as an opacity that resists all final illumination, then this seems to be a consequence of my fundamental relation to a "you"—an other who is interiorized in ways for which I can give no account. If I am first addressed and then my address emerges as a consequence, animated by a primary address and bearing the enigma of that address, then I speak to you, but you are also what is opaque in the act of my speaking. Whoever you are, you constitute me fundamentally and become the name for a primary impressionability, for the uncertain boundary between an impression from outside that I register and some consequent sense of "me" that is the site of that registering. Within this founding scene, the very grammar of the self has not yet taken hold. And so one might say, reflectively, and with a certain sense of humility, that in the beginning *I am my relation to you*, ambiguously addressed and addressing, given over to a "you" without whom I cannot be and upon whom I depend to survive.

There is no difference then between the touch and the sign that receives me and the self that I am, because the boundary is yet to be installed, the boundary between that other and this "I"—and, hence, the condition of their very possibility—is yet to take place. The self that I am yet to be (at the point where grammar does not yet permit an "I") is at the outset enthralled, even if to a scene of violence, an abandonment, a destitution, a mechanism of life support, since it is, for better or worse, the support without which I cannot be, upon which my very being depends, which my very being, fundamentally and with an irreducible ambiguity, *is*. This is a scene, if we can call it that, to which we return, within which our action takes place, and which gently or perhaps violently mocks the posture of narrative control. One can attempt to cover it over; indeed, the enunciated "I" may well function as that covering. To ward off the emergence of this opacity, it may be that no action is taken: To act is immediately to break the narrative structure and so to risk losing a self over whom I maintain narrative control. Indeed, I maintain narrative control in order to stave off a threat of dissolution, which "acting" might well precipitate or which I am convinced would definitely be precipitated.

And yet, to tell the story of oneself is already to act, since telling is a kind of action, performed with some addressee, generalized or specific, as an implied feature. It is an action in the direction of an other, as well as an action that requires an other, in which an other is presupposed. The other is thus within the action of my telling; it is not simply a question of imparting information *to* an other who is over there, beyond me, waiting to know. On the contrary, the telling performs an action that presupposes an Other, posits and elaborates the other, is given to the other, or by virtue of the other, prior to the giving of any information. So if, at the beginning—and we must laugh here, since we cannot narrate that beginning with any kind of authority, indeed, such a narration is the occasion in which we lose whatever narrative authority we might otherwise enjoy—*I am only in the address to you*, then the "I" that I am is nothing without this "you," and cannot even begin to refer to itself outside the relation to the other by which its capacity for self-reference emerges. I am mired, given over, and even the word *dependency* cannot do the job here. This means that I am also formed in ways that precede and enable my self-forming; this particular kind of transitivity is difficult, if not impossible, to narrate.

It will be necessary to reconsider the relationship of ethics to social critique, since part of what I find so hard to narrate are the norms— social in character—that bring me into being. They are, as it were, the condition of my speech, but I cannot fully thematize these conditions within the terms of my speech. I am interrupted by my own social origin, and so have to find a way to take stock of who I am in a way that makes clear that I am authored by what precedes and exceeds me, and that this in no way exonerates me from having to give an account of myself. But it does mean that if I posture as if I could reconstruct the norms by which my status as a subject is installed and maintained, then I refuse the very disorientation and interruption of my narrative that the social dimension of those norms imply. This does not mean that I cannot speak of such matters, but only that when I do, I must be careful to understand the limits of what I can do, the limits that condition any and all such doing. In this sense, I must become critical.

THREE

Responsibility

The corporeality of one's own body signifies, as sensibility itself, a knot or
denouement of being . . . a knot that cannot be undone.

—Levinas, *Otherwise than Being*

So, according to the kind of theory I have been pursuing here, what
will responsibility look like? Haven't we, by insisting on something
non-narrativizable, limited the degree to which we might hold ourselves or others accountable for their actions? I want to suggest that
the very meaning of responsibility must be rethought on the basis of
this limitation; it cannot be tied to the conceit of a self fully transparent to itself.[1] Indeed, to take responsibility for oneself is to avow
the limits of any self-understanding, and to establish these limits not
only as a condition for the subject but as the predicament of the
human community. I am not altogether out of the loop of the Enlightenment if I say, as I do, that reason's limit is the sign of our
humanity. It might even be a legacy of Kant to say so. My account
of myself breaks down, and surely for a reason, but that does not
mean that I can supply all the reasons that would make my account
whole. Reasons course through me that I cannot fully recuperate,
that remain enigmatic, that abide with me as my own familiar alter-

ity, my own private, or not so private, opacity. I speak as an "I," but do not make the mistake of thinking that I know precisely all that I am doing when I speak in that way. I find that my very formation implicates the other in me, that my own foreignness to myself is, paradoxically, the source of my ethical connection with others. Do I need to know myself in order to act responsibly in social relations? Surely, to a certain extent, yes. But is there an ethical valence to my unknowingness? If I am wounded, I find that the wound testifies to the fact that I am impressionable, given over to the other in ways that I cannot fully predict or control. I cannot think the question of responsibility alone, in isolation from the other. If I do, I have taken myself out of the mode of address (being addressed as well as addressing the other) in which the problem of responsibility first emerges.

This is not to say that one cannot be addressed in a harmful way. Or that being addressed is not sometimes traumatic. For Laplanche, the primary address overwhelms: It cannot be interpreted or understood. It is the primary experience of trauma. To be addressed carries with it a trauma, resonates with the traumatic, and yet this trauma can be experienced only belatedly through a *second* occurrence. Another word comes our way, a blow, an address or naming that suddenly, inexplicably slaughters, even as one lives on, strangely, as this slaughtered being, speaking away.

Laplanche and Levinas: The Primacy of the Other

> Levinas speaks of the subjectivity of the subject. If one wishes to use this word—why? But why not?—one ought perhaps to speak of a subjectivity without a subject: the wounded space, the hurt of the dying, the already dead body which no one could ever own, or ever say of it, *I, my body.*
>
> —Maurice Blanchot, *The Writing of the Disaster*

Given that we are vulnerable to the address of others in ways that we cannot fully control, no more than we can control the sphere of language, does this mean that we are without agency and without responsibility? For Levinas, who separates the claim of responsibility from the possibility of agency, responsibility emerges as a consequence of being subject to the unwilled address of the other. This is part of what he means when he claims, maddeningly, that persecution creates a responsibility *for the persecuted.* Most people recoil in horror when they first hear this kind of statement, but let us consider carefully what it does and does not mean. It does *not* mean that I can trace the acts of persecution I have suffered to deeds I have performed, that it therefore follows that I have brought persecution on myself, and that it is only a matter of finding the acts I performed, but disavowed. No, persecution is precisely what happens *without the warrant of any deed of my own.* And it returns us not to our acts and choices but to the region of existence that is radically unwilled, the primary, inaugurating impingement on me by the Other, one that happens to me, paradoxically, in advance of my formation as a "me"or, rather, as the instrument of that first formation of myself in the accusative case.

Levinas considers the accusative inauguration of the *moi*—the "me"—in both its grammatical and ethical senses. Only through a certain accusation does the "me" emerge. In this sense, paradoxically, he is aligned with Nietzsche, for whom the accusation of guilt produces the possibility of a subject. For Nietzsche, the subject emerges through a retroactive understanding of itself as the cause of an injury and proceeds to punish itself, thus spawning a reflexivity in which the "I" first treats itself as an object, a "me." For Levinas, though, responsibility does *not* emerge as self-preoccupation or self-beratement, and it requires recourse to an understanding of the ethical relation to the Other that does not rely on causal links between a doer and a deed.

In *Otherwise than Being,* Levinas makes clear that, before we can speak about a self who is capable of choice, we must first consider how that self is formed. This formation takes place, in his words, "outside of being [*essence*]." Indeed, the sphere in which the subject is said to emerge is "preontological" in the sense that the phenomenal world of persons and things becomes available only after a self has been formed as an effect of a primary impingement. We cannot ask after the "where" or "when" of this primary scene, since it precedes and even conditions the spatio-temporal coordinates that circumscribe the ontological domain. To describe this scene is to take leave of the descriptive field in which a "self" is formed and bounded in one place and time and considers its "objects" and "others" in their locatedness elsewhere. The possibility of this epistemological encounter presumes that the self and its object world have already been constituted, but such an encounter fails to inquire into the mechanism of that constitution. Levinas's concept of the preontological is designed to address this problem.

For Levinas, no "ego" or *moi* is inaugurated by its own acts, which means that he fully disputes the existential account proffered by Sartre: "prior to the ego taking a decision, the outside of being, where the Ego arises or is accused, is necessary." The sense of "accusation" here will become available to us soon, but let us consider how Levinas explains this primary moment or scene. The ego arises, he tells us:

> through an unlimited susceptibility, anarchical and *without assumption*, which, unlike the susceptibility of matter determined by a cause, is overdetermined by a valuing. The birth of the Ego in a gnawing remorse, which is precisely a withdrawing into oneself; this is the absolute recurrence of substitution. The condition, or non-condition, of the Self is not originally an auto-affection presupposing the Ego but is precisely an affection by the Other, an *anarchic traumatism* [an-archic, without principle, and so assuredly, enigmatic, that for which no clear cause can be given], this side of auto-affection and self-identification, a traumatism of responsibility and not causality.[2]

We might accept Levinas's claim that the primary trauma emerges through an initial impingement by the Other—surely that is Laplanche's view—without casting this impingement as accusation. Why does this traumatism, this affection by the Other, arrive for Levinas in the form of an accusation and a persecution? When he writes that "persecution is the precise moment where the subject is reached or touched without the mediation of the logos" (S, 93), he is referring once again to this "preontological" scene in which the subject is inaugurated, as it were, through a persecutory "reach" or "touch" that works without consciousness, without cause, and according to no principle. We have to ask why this is understood as persecution or, rather, what Levinas is trying to tell us about what persecution is. A passive relation to other beings precedes the formation of the ego or the *moi* or, put slightly differently, becomes the instrument through which that formation takes place. A formation in passivity, then, constitutes the prehistory of the subject, instating an ego as object, acted on by others, prior to any possibility of its own acting. This scene is persecutory because it is unwilled and unchosen. It is a way of being acted on prior to the possibility of acting oneself or in one's own name.

Just as Laplanche warns us that the story he tells about primary repression, the formation of drives and the "I," has to be speculative, so Levinas cautions us against thinking we can find a narrative form for this preontological beginning. Levinas writes, "The upsurge of the oneself in persecution, the anarchic passivity of substitution, is not some event whose history we might recount, but a conjunction which describes the ego . . . subject to being, subject to every being" (S, 90). This passivity, what Levinas calls "a passivity before passivity," has to be understood not as the opposite of activity but as the precondition for the active-passive distinction as it arises in grammar and in everyday descriptions of interactions within the established field of ontology. What cross-cuts this field of ontology synchronically is the preontological condition of a passivity for which no conversion into its opposite is possible. To understand this, we must think of a susceptibility to others that is unwilled, unchosen, that is a condition of our responsiveness to others, even a condition of our responsibility *for* them. It means, among other things, that this susceptibility designates a nonfreedom and, paradoxically, it is on the basis of this susceptibility over which we have no choice that we become responsible for others.

Of course, it is not easy at first to understand how Levinas moves from the claim that humans have toward others a radically unchosen "preontological" susceptibility to the claim that this susceptibility forms the basis of our responsibility toward others. He admits quite clearly that this primary susceptibility is a "persecution" precisely because it is unwilled, because we are radically subject to another's action upon us, and because there is no possibility of replacing this susceptibility with an act of will or an exercise of freedom. We are used to thinking that we can be responsible only for that which we have done, that which can be traced to our intentions, our deeds. Levinas explicitly rejects this view, claiming that tethering responsibility to freedom is an error. I become responsible by virtue of what is done to me, but I do not become responsible for what is done to me if by "responsibility" we mean blaming myself for the outrages done to me. On the contrary, I am *not* primarily responsible by virtue of my actions, but by virtue of the relation to the Other that is established at the level of my primary and irreversible susceptibility, my passivity prior to any possibility of action or choice.

Levinas explains that responsibility in this instance is neither a kind of self-beratement nor a grandiose concept of my own actions as the sole causal effect on others. Rather, my capacity to be *acted upon* implicates me in a relation of responsibility. This happens by way of what Levinas calls "substitution," whereby the "I" is understood as beset by an Other, an alterity, from the start. He writes,

> here it is not a question of humiliating oneself, as if suffering were in itself . . . a magical power of atonement. But because, in suffering, in the *original traumatism* and return to self, where I am respon-

sible for what I did not will, absolutely responsible for the persecution I undergo, outrage is done to me. (S, 90)

He goes on to describe the self to whom outrage is done as backed up "to the point of being substituted for all that drives you into this non-Place" (S, 90). Something drives me that is not me, and the "me" arises precisely in the experience of, and as the effect of, being driven in this way. The absolute passivity of "being driven" is a kind of persecution and outrage, not because I am treated *badly*, but because I am treated *unilaterally*; the pre-emergent "I" that I am is nothing more at this point than a radical susceptibility subject to impingement by the Other. If I become responsible only through being acted on by an Other, that is because the "I" first comes into being as a "me" through being acted upon by an Other, and this primary impingement is already and from the start an ethical interpellation.

How does substitution come into the picture? It would seem that what persecutes me comes to substitute for the "I." That which persecutes me brings me into being, acts upon me, and so prompts me, animates me into ontology at the moment of persecution. This suggests not only that I am acted upon unilaterally from the outside but that this "acting upon" inaugurates a sense of me that is, from the outset, a sense of the Other. I am acted on as the accusative object of the Other's action, and my self first takes form within that accusation. The form that persecution takes is substitution itself: something places itself in my place, and an "I" emerges who can understand its place in no other way than as this place already occupied by another. In the beginning, then, I am not only persecuted but besieged, occupied.

If something substitutes for me or takes my place, that means neither that it comes to exist where I once was, nor that I no longer am, nor that I have been resolved into nothingness by virtue of being replaced in some way. Rather, substitution implies that an irreducible transitivity, substitution, which is no single act, is happening all the time (*OB*, 117). Whereas "persecution" suggests that something acts on me from the outside, 'substitution' suggests that something takes my place or, better, is always in the process of taking my place. "Being held hostage" implies that something encircles me, impinging in a way that does not let me get free. It even raises the possibility that there may be a ransom for me that someone somewhere must pay (but unfortunately, in a Kafkaesque vein, that person no longer exists or the currency at one's disposal has become obsolete).

It is important to note here that Levinas is not saying that primary relations are abusive or terrible; he is simply saying that at the most primary level we are acted upon by others in ways over which we have no say, and that this passivity, susceptibility, and condition of *being impinged upon* inaugurate who we are. Levinas's references to sub-ject formation do not refer to a childhood (Laplanche seems right that childhood would not factor for Levinas) and is given no dia-chronic exposition; the condition is, rather, understood as synchronic and infinitely recurring.

Most importantly, this condition of being impinged upon is also an "address" of a certain kind. One can argue that it is the voice of no one, the voice of a God, understood as infinite and preontological, that makes itself known in the "face" of the Other. That would surely conform to many of Levinas's own claims about the primary address. For our purposes, however, we will treat the Other in Levi-nas as belonging to an idealized dyadic structure of social life. The other's actions "address" me in the sense that those actions belong to an Other who is irreducible, whose "face" makes an ethical de-mand upon me. We might say, "even the Other who brutalizes me has a face," and that would capture the difficulty of remaining ethi-cally responsive to those who do injury to us. For Levinas, however, the demand is even greater: "precisely the Other who persecutes me has a face." Moreover, the face is turned toward me, individuating me through its address. Whereas the Other's action upon me (re)inaugurates me through substitutability, the Other's face, we might say, addresses me in a way that is singular, irreducible, and irreplaceable. Thus responsibility emerges not with the "I" but with the accusative "me": "Who finally takes on the suffering of others, if not the being who says, 'Me' [*Moi*]?'"[3]

It makes sense to assume that this primary susceptibility to the action and the face of the other, the full ambivalence of an unwanted address, is what constitutes our exposure to injury *and* our responsibility for the Other. This susceptibility is an ethical resource precisely because it establishes our vulnerability or exposure to what Levinas calls "wounds and outrages." These feelings are, in his view, "proper to responsibility itself." Importantly, the condition of substitution that brings us into being nevertheless establishes us as singular and irreplaceable in relation to the ethical demand placed upon us by others: "the oneself is provoked as irreplaceable, as devoted to the others, without being able to resign, and thus as incarnated in order to offer itself, to suffer and to give"(*OB*, 105).

If it were not for this exposure to outrage, we could not respond to the demand to assume responsibility for the Other. It is important to remember that our ordinary way of thinking about responsibility is altered in Levinas's formulation. *We do not take responsibility for the Other's acts as if we authored those acts.* On the contrary, we affirm the unfreedom at the heart of our relations. I cannot disavow my relation to the Other, regardless of what the Other does, regardless of what I might will. Indeed, responsibility is not a matter of cultivating a will, but of making use of an unwilled susceptibility as a resource for becoming responsive to the Other. Whatever the Other has done, the Other still makes an ethical demand upon me, has a "face" to which I am obligated to respond—meaning that I am, as it were, precluded from revenge by virtue of a relation I never chose.

It is, in some ways, an outrage to be ethically responsible for one whom one does not choose. Here, however, Levinas draws attention to lines of responsibility that precede and subtend any possible choice. There are situations in which responding to the "face" of the other feels horrible, impossible, and where the desire for murderous revenge feels overwhelming. But the primary and unwilled relation to the Other demands that we desist from both a voluntarism and an impulsive aggression grounded in the self-preservative aims of egoism. The "face" thus communicates an enormous prohibition against aggression directed toward the persecutor. In "Ethics and Spirit," Levinas writes:

> The face, for its part, is inviolable; those eyes, which are absolutely without protection, the most naked part of the human body, nonetheless offer an absolute resistance to possession, an absolute resistance in which the temptation to murder is inscribed. . . . The Other is the only being that one can be tempted to kill. This temptation to murder and this impossibility of murder constitute the very vision of the face. To see a face is already to hear "You shall not kill," and to hear "You shall not kill" is to hear "social justice." (*DF*, 8)

If "persecution" by the Other refers to the range of actions that are unilaterally imposed upon us without our will, the term takes on a more literal meaning for Levinas when he speaks of injuries and, finally, of the Nazi genocide. Levinas writes, amazingly, that "in the trauma of persecution" the ethical consists in "pass[ing] from the outrage undergone to the responsibility for the persecutor . . . from suffering to expiation for the other" (*OB*, 111). Responsibility thus arises as a demand upon the persecuted, and its central dilemma is whether or not one may kill in response to persecution. It is, we might say, the limit case of the prohibition against killing, the condition under which its justification would seem most reasonable. In 1971, Levinas reflects upon the meaning that the Holocaust has for his reflections on persecution and responsibility. He is surely aware that to derive responsibility from persecution echoes perilously with those who would blame the Jews and other victims of the Nazi genocide for their fates. Levinas clearly rejects this view. He does, however, establish persecution as a certain kind of ethical demand and opportunity. He situates the particular nexus of persecution and responsibility at the core of Judaism, even as the essence of Israel. By "Israel" he refers ambiguously to both senses of the word, the Jewish people and the land of Palestine. He maintains, controversially, that

> The ultimate essence of Israel derives from its innate [*innée*] predisposition to involuntary sacrifice, its exposure to persecution. Not that we need think of the mystical expiation that it would fulfill like a host. To be persecuted, to be guilty without having committed any crime, is not an original sin, but the obverse of a universal responsibility—a responsibility for the Other [*l'Autre*]—that is more ancient than any sin. It is an invisible universality! It is the reverse of a choosing that puts forward the *self* [moi] before it is even free to accept being chosen. It is *for the others* to see if they wish to take advantage of it [*abuser*]. It is for the free *self* [moi *libre*] to fix the limits of this responsibility or to claim entire responsibility. But it can do so only in the name of that original responsibility, in the name of this Judaism. (*DF*, 225)

This paragraph is complex and problematic for many reasons, not least of which is the direct link Levinas draws between the suffering of the Jews under Nazism and the suffering of Israel, understood as land and as people, from 1948 to 1971, the time of his writing. That the fate of Israel is equated with the fate of the Jews is controversial in its own right, dismissing both diasporic and non-Zionist traditions in Judaism. More emphatically, it is clearly wrong to claim that the state of Israel *only* suffered persecution during those years, given the massive and forcible displacement of more than seven hundred thousand Palestinians from their homes and villages in 1948 alone, not to mention the destitutions of the continuing war and occupation. It is curious that Levinas should here extract "persecution" from its concrete historical appearances, establishing it as an apparently timeless essence of Judaism. If this were true, then any historical argument to the contrary could be refuted on definitional grounds alone: "Jews cannot be persecutory since, by definition, Jews are the persecuted." This attribution of persecution to what "Israel" suffers dovetails with his view of the preontological structure of the subject. If Jews are considered "elect" because they carry a message of universality, and what is "universal" in Levinas's view is the inaugurative structuring of the subject through persecution and ethical demand, then the Jew becomes the model and instance for preontological persecution. The problem, of course, is that "the Jew" is a category that belongs to a culturally constituted ontology (unless it is the name for access to the infinite itself), and so if the Jew maintains an "elective" status in relation to ethical responsiveness, then Levinas fully confuses the preontological and the ontological. The Jew is not part of ontology or history, and yet this exemption becomes the way in which Levinas makes claims about the role of Israel, historically considered, as forever and exclusively persecuted. The same confusion between the two domains is made clear in other contexts where, with blatant racism, Levinas claims that Judaism and Christianity are the cultural and religious preconditions of ethical relationality itself and warns against the "rise of the countless masses of Asiatic [*des masses innombrables des peuples asiatiques*] and underdeveloped peoples [who] threaten[] the new-found authenticity" (*DF*, 165) of Jewish universalism. This, in turn, resonates with his warning that ethics cannot be based on "exotic cultures."

I won't reveal my full quarrel with his argument here (which is complex and tenacious), but I want to underline that a vacillation exists for Levinas between the preontological sense of *persecution*— associated with an impingement that takes place prior to any ontology—and a fully ontological sense that comes to define the "essence" of a people. Similarly, through apposition at the end of the paragraph, "the name of original responsibility" is aligned with "the name of this Judaism," at which point it seems clear that this original and, hence, preontological responsibility is the same as the essence of Judaism. For this to be a distinguishing feature of Judaism in particular, it cannot be a distinguishing feature of all religions, and he makes this clear when he cautions against all religious traditions that fail to refer to the history of the saints and to Abraham, Isaac, and Jacob (*DF*, 165). Although in his rendition we receive an implausible and outrageous account of the Jewish people problematically identified with Israel and figured only as persecuted and never persecuting, it is possible to read his account against himself, as it were, and arrive at a different conclusion. Indeed, Levinas's words here carry wounds and outrages, and they pose an ethical dilemma for those who read them. Although he would circumscribe a given religious tradition as the precondition for ethical responsibility, thereby casting other traditions as threats to ethicality, it makes sense for us to insist, as it were, on a face-to-face encounter precisely here where Levinas claims it cannot be done. Moreover, although he wounds us here or, perhaps, precisely because he wounds us, we are responsible for him, even as the relation proves painful in its nonreciprocity.

To be persecuted, he tells us, is the obverse of a responsibility for the Other. The two are linked fundamentally, and we see the objective correlate of this in the double valence of the face: "This temptation to murder and this impossibility of murder constitute the very vision of the face." To be persecuted can lead to murder in response, even the displacement of murderous aggression onto those who in no way authored the injuries for which one seeks revenge. But for Levinas an ethical demand emerges precisely from the humanization of the face: This one I am tempted to murder in self-defense is a "one" who makes a claim upon me, preventing me from becoming the persecutor in reverse. It is, of course, one thing to argue that responsibility arises from the situation of being persecuted—that is a compelling and counter-intuitive claim, especially if responsibility does not mean identifying oneself as the cause of another's injurious action. But to argue that any historically constituted group of people are, by definition, always persecuted and never persecutory seems not only to confound the ontological and preontological levels but to license an unacceptable irresponsibility and a limitless recourse to aggression in the name of "self-defense." Indeed, the Jews have a culturally complex history that includes the sufferings of anti-semitism, pogroms, and concentration camps where over six million were slaughtered. But there is also the history of religious and cultural traditions that exist, many of which are pre-Zionist, and there is a history, more vexed than is usually acknowledged, of a relation to Israel as a complex ideal. To say that persecution is the essence of Judaism not only overrides agency and aggression performed in the name of Judaism but preempts a cultural and historical analysis that would have to be complex and specific through recourse to a singular preontological condition, one that, understood as universal, is identified as the transhistorical and defining truth of the Jewish people.

The "preontological" domain to which Levinas refers (of which he says any representation would be a "betrayal") is difficult to conjure, since it would seem to surge up into the ontological, where it leaves its traces. Any finite representation betrays the infinity represented, but representations do carry the trace of the infinite. The "inauguration" of the subject takes place through the impingement by which an infinite ethical demand is communicated. But this scene cannot be narrated in time; it recurs throughout time and belongs to an order other than that of time. It is interesting, on this point, to recall Laplanche's brief criticism of Levinas. That centers on the inability of the Levinasian position to give an account of the diachronic formation of the human subject. Whereas Levinas accounts for the inauguration of the "me" through a primary and synchronically conceived scene of preontological impingement, Laplanche considers the infant, primary repression, the formation of object-sources that become the internal generator of drives and their recurrent opacity. For both, though, the *primat* or impress of the Other is primary, inaugurative, and there is no formation of a "me" outside of this originally passive impingement and the responsiveness formed in the crucible of that passivity.

Laplanche's infant is "overwhelmed" by a generalized seduction imposed by the sexualized adult world, unable to receive sexual "messages" that, in their enigmatic and incomprehensible form, become interiorized as an opaque dynamism in its own most primary impulses. The enigmatic sexual demand of the adult world resurfaces as the enigmatic sexual demand of my own impulses or drives. The drives are formed as a consequence of this impingement by the world, so there is no ready-made ego equipped with its own internal drives: There is only an interiority and an ego produced as the effect of an interiorization of the enigmatic signifiers that emerge in the broader cultural world. Levinas's "me" emerges not through seduction but through accusation and persecution, and though a possibility for murderous aggression is constituted in response to this scenario, it is twinned with an ethical responsiveness that seems to be there from the start, a constitutive feature of a primary human susceptibility to the Other.

The Levinasian position is not, finally, compatible with a psychoanalytic one, even though it might appear that this primary persecution parallels Laplanche's notion of a primary address that overwhelms. Laplanche maintains that the unconscious cannot be understood as "my" unconscious, as something predicated upon an already-existing me, something that can be converted into consciousness or, indeed, the ego. This seems not to square with the caricature of psychoanalysis that Levinas offers, especially when he goes on to say that the positing of the unconscious will not do. We might expect what he says to take care of the kind of position we have been reading about in Laplanche. "The hither side" of consciousness is not the unconscious, Levinas remarks, "the unconscious, in its clandestinity, rehearses the game played out in consciousness, namely, the search for meaning and truth as the search for the self" (S, 83). For Laplanche, there is no restoration of self-consciousness. For Laplanche, surely, there is no conversion of the id or the unconscious into ego or consciousness, and this remains the core of his struggle with forms of ego psychology that seek precisely those goals. Self-consciousness is always driven, quite literally, by an alterity that has become internal, a set of enigmatic signifiers that pulse through us in ways that make us permanently and partially foreign to ourselves.

Although Laplanche and Levinas both subscribe to notions of primary passivity and identify the Other at the inception of the "me," the differences between them are significant. If we look closely at Laplanche's account of the drive, for instance, we find that it is initiated and structured by the enigmatic signifier. We are not able to determine with clarity whether the drive is already at work when the primary trauma takes place. But displacement seems to take place only by virtue of trauma, and that displacement inaugurates the drive and separates it from its minimum biological condition, understood as "instinct."[4] If for Laplanche there is a primary helplessness in the face of enigmatic sexual messages relayed from the adult world, and this precipitates a primary repression and the internalization of the enigmatic signifier, then it would seem that this primary impression-ability is not only "passive." It is, rather, helpless, anxious, frightened, overwhelmed and, finally, desirous. There is, in other words, a range of affective response that happens at the moment that an impinge-ment takes place.

Levinas cannot accommodate the notion of a primary set of needs or drives, though he gestures toward an elementary notion of aggression or murderous impulse when he grants that killing the Other is the temptation against which ethics must work. For Laplanche and Levinas, though, these primary affects, whether aggression or the drive, are consequences of a prior impingement by the Other, and so are always "secondary" in that sense. Whereas Levinas asserts a primary passivity indissolubly linked with an ethical responsiveness,

Laplanche maintains that there is a primary indissolubility of impression and drive. For Laplanche, the adult world delivers messages that are overwhelmingly enigmatic for children, producing a sense of helplessness and instigating a desire for mastery. But these messages are not simply imprinted. They are registered, taken up by the drive, and enter into the subsequent forms that the drive assumes. This is tricky territory, since it would be a mistake to hold children responsible for the messages that they receive. Those messages always first arrive unsolicited by an infant or a child. Yet it becomes the struggle, the task of the emergent person, to make sense of them, to find a place for them, and later in adulthood to come to terms with the fact that they have registered at levels that are not fully recoverable by consciousness.

Can we say that the experience of being imposed upon from the start, against one's will, heightens a sense of responsibility? Have we perhaps unwittingly destroyed the possibility for agency with all this talk about being given over, being structured, being addressed? In adult experience, we no doubt suffer all kinds of injuries, even violations. These expose something of a primary vulnerability and impressionability and may well recall primary experiences in more or less traumatic ways. Do such experiences form the basis for a sense of responsibility? In what sense can we understand a heightened sense of responsibility to emerge from the experience of injury or violation?

Let us consider for a moment that by "responsibility" I do not mean a heightened moral sense that consists simply in an internalization of rage and a shoring up of the superego. Nor am I referring to a sense of guilt that seeks to find a cause in oneself for what one has suffered. These are surely possible and prevalent responses to injury and violence, but they are all responses that heighten reflexivity, shoring up the subject, its claims to self-sufficiency, its centrality and indispensability to the field of its experience. Bad conscience is a form of negative narcissism, as both Freud and Nietzsche have told us in different ways. And, being a form of narcissism, it recoils from the other, from impressionability, susceptibility, and vulnerability. The myriad forms of bad conscience that Freud and Nietzsche analyze so deftly show us that moralizing forms of subjectivity harness and exploit the very impulses they seek to curb. Moreover, they show that the very instrument of repression is wrought from those impulses, creating a tautological circuitry in which impulse feeds the very law by which it is prohibited. But is there a theorization of responsibility beyond bad conscience? To the extent that bad conscience withdraws the subject into narcissism, to what degree does it work against responsibility, precisely because it forecloses the primary relation to alterity by which we are animated, and from which the possibility of ethical responsiveness emerges?

What might it mean to undergo violation, to insist upon *not* resolving grief and staunching vulnerability too quickly through a turn to violence, and to practice, as an experiment in living otherwise, nonviolence in an emphatically nonreciprocal response? What would it mean, in the face of violence, to refuse to return it? Perhaps we might have to think, along with Levinas, that self-preservation is not the highest goal, and the defense of a narcissistic point of view not the most urgent psychic need. That we are impinged upon primarily and against our will is the sign of a vulnerability and a beholdenness that we cannot will away. We can defend against it only by prizing the asociality of the subject over and against a difficult and intractable, even sometimes unbearable relationality. What might it mean to make an ethic from the region of the unwilled? It might mean that one does not foreclose upon that primary exposure to the Other, that one does not try to transform the unwilled into the willed, but, rather, to take the very unbearability of exposure as the sign, the reminder, of a common vulnerability, a common physicality and risk (even as "common" does not mean "symmetrical" for Levinas).

It is always possible to say, "Oh, some violence was done to me, and this gives me full permission to act under the sign of 'self-defense.'" Many atrocities are committed under the sign of a "self-defense" that, precisely because it achieves a permanent moral justification for retaliation, knows no end and can have no end. Such a strategy has developed an infinite way to rename its aggression as suffering and so provides an infinite justification for its aggression. Or it is possible to say that "I" or "we" have brought this violence upon ourselves, and thus to account for it by recourse to our deeds, as if we believed in their omnipotence, believed that our own deeds are the cause of all possible effects. Indeed, guilt of this sort exacerbates our sense of omnipotence, sometimes under the very sign of its critique. Violence is neither a just punishment we suffer nor a just revenge for what we suffer. It delineates a physical vulnerability from which we cannot slip away, which we cannot finally resolve in the name of the subject, but which can provide a way to understand that none of us is fully bounded, utterly separate, but, rather, we are in our skins, given over, in each other's hands, at each other's mercy. This is a situation we do not choose. It forms the horizon of choice, and it grounds our responsibility. In this sense, we are not responsible for it, but it creates the conditions under which we assume responsibility. We did not create it, and therefore it is what we must heed.

Adorno on Becoming Human

> The secret of justice in love is the annulment of all rights, to which love mutely points.
>
> —Adorno, *Minima Moralia*

The way in which we respond to injury may offer a chance to elaborate an ethical perspective and even become human. Adorno takes up this point in various ways. He seems to be talking about private ethics in the following quotation from *Minima Moralia*, but there are wider political implications to what he writes:

> Someone who has been offended, slighted, has an illumination as vivid as when agonizing pain lights up one's own body. He be-

comes aware that in the innermost blindness of love, that must remain oblivious, lives a demand not to be blinded. He was wronged; from this he deduces a claim to right and must at the same time reject it, for what he desires can only be given in freedom. In such distress he who is rebuffed becomes human.[5]

A claim that "in such distress he who is rebuffed becomes human" might seem to rationalize injury or to praise its virtues. But I think neither Adorno nor Levinas is engaged in such praise.[6] Rather, they accept the inevitability of injury, along with a moral predicament that emerges as a consequence of being injured. Over and against those who would claim that ethics is the prerogative of the powerful, one might counter that only from the viewpoint of the injured can a certain conception of responsibility be understood. What will be the response to injury, and will we, in the language of a cautionary political slogan on the left, "become the evil that we deplore"? If, as Adorno remarks, "in the innermost blindness of love . . . lives a demand not to be blinded," then the blindness of love would seem to correspond to the primacy of enthrallment, to the fact that from the outset we are implicated in a mode of relationality that cannot be fully thematized, subject to reflection, and cognitively known. This mode of relationality, definitionally blind, makes us vulnerable to betrayal and to error. We could wish ourselves to be wholly perspicacious beings. But that would be to disavow infancy, dependency, relationality, primary impressionability; it would be the wish to eradicate all the active and structuring traces of our psychological formations and to dwell in the pretense of being fully knowing, self-possessed adults. Indeed, we would be the kind of beings who, by definition, could not be in love, blind and blinded, vulnerable to devastation, subject to enthrallment. If we were to respond to injury by claiming we had a "right" not to be so treated, we would be treating the other's love as an entitlement rather than a gift. Being a gift, it carries the insuperable quality of gratuitousness. It is, in Adorno's language, a gift given from freedom.

But is the alternative contract or freedom? Or, just as no contract can guarantee us love, might it be equally mistaken to conclude that love is therefore given in a radically free sense? Indeed, the unfreedom at the heart of love does not belong to contract. After all, the love of the other will, of necessity, be blind even in its knowingness. That we are compelled in love means that we are, in part, unknowing about why we love as we do and why we invariably exercise bad judgment. Very often what we call "love" involves being compelled by our own opacity, our own places of unknowingness, and, indeed, our own injury (which is why, for instance, Melanie Klein will insist that fantasies of reparation structure love). In the passage above, however, Adorno traces a movement in which one is compelled to claim a right not to be rebuffed and resists making the claim at the same time. It is possible to read this as a paralyzing contradiction, but I think that this is not what he means to imply. Rather, it is a model of ethical capaciousness, which understands the pull of the claim and resists that pull at the same time, providing a certain am-bivalent gesture as the action of ethics itself. One seeks to preserve oneself against the injuriousness of the other, but if one were success-ful at walling oneself off from injury, one would become inhuman. In this sense, we make a mistake when we take "self-preservation" to be the essence of the human, unless we accordingly claim that the "inhuman" is constitutive of the human. One of the problems with insisting on self-preservation as the basis of ethics is that it becomes a pure ethics of the self, if not a form of moral narcissism. Persisting in the vacillation between wanting to claim a right against such injury and resisting that claim, one "becomes human."

As you can see, "becoming human" is no simple task, and it is not always clear when or if one arrives. To be human seems to mean being in a predicament that one cannot solve. In fact, Adorno makes clear that he cannot define the human for us. If the human is any-thing, it seems to be a double movement, one in which we assert moral norms at the same time as we question the authority by which we make that assertion. In his final lecture on morality, Adorno writes, "We need to hold fast to moral norms, to self-criticism, to the question of right and wrong, and at the same time to a sense of the fallibility [*Fehlbarkeit*] of the authority that has the confidence to undertake such self-criticism"(*PMP*, 169). Immediately after, he states that, although he seems to be talking about morality, he is also articulating the meaning of the human:

> I am reluctant to use the term "humanity" at this juncture since it is one of the expressions that reify and hence falsify crucial issues merely by speaking of them. When the founders of the Humanist Union invited me to become a member, I replied that 'I might possibly be willing to join if your club had been called an inhuman union, but I could not join one that calls itself 'humanist.'" So if I am to use the term here then an indispensable part of a humanity that reflects on itself is that we should not allow ourselves to be diverted. There has to be an element of unswerving persistence [*Unbeirrbarkeit*], of holding fast to what we think we have learnt from experience, and on the other hand, we need an element not just of self-criticism, but of criticism of that unyielding, inexorable something (*an jenem Starren und Unerbittlichen*), that sets itself up in us. In other words, what is needed above all is that consciousness of our own fallibility. (*PMP*, 169)

So there is something unyielding that sets itself up in us, that takes up residence within us, that constitutes what we do not know, and that renders us fallible. On the one hand, we could say as a matter of fact that every human must contend with his or her fallibility. But Adorno seems to be suggesting that something about this fallibility makes it difficult to speak about the human, to claim the human, and that it might rather be understood as "the inhuman." When he writes, a few lines later, "true injustice is always to be found at the precise point where you put yourself in the right and other people in the wrong"(*PMP*, 169), he situates morality on the side of restraint, of "not joining in," countering Heidegger's *Entschlos-*

senheit or resoluteness with the suggestion that morality consists in refraining from self-assertion. Kafka's Odradek figures this refutation of the early Heidegger.[7] That "creature" or "thing"—which resembles a spool of thread but seems also to be the son of the narrator, barely balances on two points, and rolls and rolls down the stairs in perpetuity—is surely a figure for the dehumanized being who is strangely animated by its dehumanization, whose laugh sounds like the "rustling of leaves," and whose human status is radically uncertain. Adorno understands this character from Kafka as conditioned by a certain commodity fetishism, in which persons have turned into objects and objects have become animated in macabre ways. Effectively, for Adorno, Odradek turns this early Heideggerian doctrine on its head, thus echoing what Marx did to Hegel, insofar as Odradek becomes a figure for the gesture that jettisons the very notion of will or *Entschlossenheit* by which the human is defined.

If the human in the early existentialist formulation is defined as self-defining and self-asserting, then self-restraint effectively deconstitutes the human. Self-assertion is, for Adorno, linked to a principle of self-preservation that, like Levinas, he questions as an ultimate moral value. After all, if self-assertion becomes the assertion of the self at the expense of any consideration of the world, of consequence, and, indeed, of others, then it feeds a "moral narcissism" whose pleasure resides in its ability to transcend the concrete world that conditions its actions and is affected by them.

Although Adorno says he might join a society that defines itself as a group for the "inhuman" and points to the inhuman figure of Odradek to offer a conception of survival and of hope, he is not, finally, championing the inhuman as an ideal. The inhuman, rather, establishes a critical point of departure for an analysis of the social conditions under which the human is constituted and deconstituted. Adorno shows that in Kafka the inhuman becomes a way to survive the current organization of "human" society, an animated living on of what has largely been devastated; in this sense, "the inhuman" facilitates an immanent critique of the human and becomes the trace or ruin through which the human lives on (*fortleben*). The "inhuman" is also a way of designating the way social forces take up residence within us, making it impossible to define ourselves in terms of free will. Lastly, the "inhuman" designates the way in which the social world impinges upon us in ways that make us invariably unknowing about ourselves. Obviously, we have to deal with the "inhuman" as we try to make our way through moral life, but this does not mean that the "inhuman" becomes, for Adorno, a new norm. On the contrary, he does not celebrate the "inhuman" and even calls for its ultimate denunciation. Countering what he takes to be the pseudo-problem of moral relativism, he writes:

> We may not know what absolute good is or the absolute norm, we may not even know what man is or the human [*das Menschliche*] or humanity [*die Humanität*]—but what the inhuman [*das Unmenschliche*] is we know very well indeed. I would say that the place of moral philosophy today lies more in the concrete denunciation of the inhuman, than in the vague [*Unverbindlichen*] and abstract attempts to situate man in his existence. (*PMP*, 175)

Adorno thus calls for the denunciation of the inhuman. He makes clear, however, that the inhuman is precisely what is needed to become human. After all, if being exposed to the rebuff of the other compels us to assert a right, which we must also refrain from asserting, thereby putting into question the legitimacy of that assertion, then in the latter gesture, characterized by restraint and questioning, we embody the "inhuman" by offering a critique of the will, of assertion, and of resolve as prerequisites of the human. In this sense, the "inhuman" is not the opposite of the human but an essential means by which we become human in and through the destitution of our humanness. We might conclude that Adorno has offered another view of the human here, one in which restraining the will comes to define the human as such. We might even say that, for

Adorno, when the human is defined by will and refuses the way it is impinged upon by the world, it ceases to be human. In this sense, the denunciation of the inhuman could take place only by simultaneously denouncing one version of the human. Indeed, the only way to understand him here is to accept that any conception of the human that either defines the human by will or, alternately, robs the human of all will is a conception that cannot hold. Indeed, the "inhuman" emerges for Adorno as *both* a figure of pure will (eviscerated of vulnerability) and a figure of *no* will (reduced to destitution). If he opposes dehumanization, understood as the subjugation of humans by depriving them of will, it is not because he wants humans to be defined by will. The individualist solution that would identify the will with the defining norm of humanness not only cuts the individual off from the world but destroys the basis for a moral engagement with that world. It becomes difficult here to condemn violent impingement upon the will without espousing the will as the defining condition of the human. Indeed, impingement is inevitable: there is no "right" we might assert against this fundamental condition. At the same time, surely we can, and must, devise norms to adjudicate among forms of impingement, distinguishing between its inevitable and insuperable dimension, on the one hand, and its socially contingent and reversible conditions, on the other.

Even Adorno's own "denunciation" of the inhuman turns out to be equivocal, since he also requires this term for his conception of the human. When he calls for its denunciation, he occupies the morally certain stance of one who *knows* precisely what to condemn. And at the moment that he condemns the "inhuman," he associates it with the kinds of dehumanizations he opposes. But there are clearly other forms of dehumanization that he favors, especially when they involve a critique of the will and the acknowledgment of a historically constituted sociality. Indeed, denunciation seems to be a willful act characteristic of the ethics of conviction, an individualist ethics, if not a fully narcissistic one. Thus Adorno, in the act of denunciation, occupies this position for us, showing, in effect, that this position will inevitably be occupied in some way. Denunciation, however, is not the only model for moral judgment in his reflections on morality. In fact, denunciation, too, belongs to the ethics of conviction rather than the ethics of responsibility, and the latter characterizes the project he pursues in his lectures on morality.

Conviction appears to belong to an ethics that takes the self to be the ground and measure of moral judgment. For Adorno, following Max Weber, responsibility has to do with assuming an action in the context of a social world where consequences matter.[8] Adorno's characterization of Kantianism as a form of moral narcissism seems to rest on this conviction, suggesting as well that any deontological position that refuses consequentialism runs the risk of devolving into narcissism and, in that sense, ratifying the social organization of individualism. According to the version of Kantianism that subscribes to "an ideal of abstract reason," the very capacity to err, to be blinded, to blind, or to commit a "life-lie" is ruled out of the conception of the human. To be true, according to Adorno's model of this Kantianism, means to follow the injunction to "be identical with yourself. And in this identity, in what might be called this reduction of moral demands to being true to oneself and nothing more, it is natural for every specific principle about how we should behave to evaporate, to the point where according to this ethics you could end up being a true man if you are a true, that is, conscious and transparent, rogue [*Schurke*]" (*PMP*, 161).

Indeed, Adorno makes the point more emphatically when he claims, with Ibsen, that forms of moral purity are often nourished by a "hidden egoism." Kant as well, he argues,

> had a sharp eye for the fact that the motives we think of as pure, and hence in conformity with the categorical imperative [*die des kategorischen Imperatives vorspiegeln*], are in truth only motives whose source lies in the empirical world. They are ultimately linked to

our faculty of desire and therefore with the gratification of what I would term our moral narcissism. We may say in general—and this is what is valid [*wahr*] about this critique—that it is right to feel a certain wariness towards people who are said to be of pure will [*die sogenannte reinen Willens*], and who take every opportunity to refer to their own purity of will. The reality is that this so-called pure will is almost always twinned [*verschwistert*] with the willingness to denounce others, with the need to punish and persecute others, in short, with the entire problematic nature of what will be all too familiar to you from the various purges [*Reinigungsaktionen*] that have taken place in totalitarian states. (*PMP*, 163)

Adorno seeks to show the dialectical inversion that takes place between moral purity and moral narcissism, between an ethics of conviction and a politics of persecution; his conceptual apparatus always assumes that the logical form these relations will take will be binary, inverse, belonging to a negative dialectic. This mode of analysis works to the degree that we accept that social relations are structured by contradiction and that the divergence between abstract principle, on the one side, and practical action, on the other, is constitutive of the historical times.

Several propositions that Adorno has laid out for us converge in some interesting and important ways with the problematic of ethics as it emerges for the late Foucault. Foucault, like Adorno, maintains that ethics can only be understood in terms of a process of critique, where critique attends, among other things, to the regimes of intelligibility that order ontology and, specifically, the ontology of the subject. When Foucault asks the question "What, given the contemporary regime of being, can I be?" he locates the possibility of subject formation in a historically instituted order of ontology maintained through coercive effects. There is no possibility of a pure and unmediated relation of myself to my will, conceived as free or not, apart from the constitution of my self, and its modes of self-observation, within a given historical ontology.

Adorno makes a slightly different point, but I think the two positions resonate with one another. Adorno claims that it makes no sense to refer in an abstract way to principles that govern behavior without referring to the consequences of any given action authorized by those principles. Our responsibility is not just for the purity of our souls but for the shape of the collectively inhabited world. This means that action has to be understood as consequential. Ethics, we might say, gives rise to critique or, rather, cannot proceed without it, since we have to become knowing about the ways in which our actions are taken up by the already-constituted social world and what consequences will follow from our acting in certain ways. Deliberation takes place in relation to a concrete set of historical circumstances, but more importantly, in relation to an understanding of the patterned ways in which action is regulated within the contemporary social horizon.

Just as Foucault objects to forms of ethics that consign the subject to an endless and self-berating preoccupation with a psyche, considered to be internal and unique, so Adorno objects to the devolution of ethics into forms of moral narcissism. Both are trying, in different ways, to dislodge the subject as the ground of ethics in order to recast the subject as a problem *for* ethics. This is not the death of the subject, in either case, but an inquiry into the modes by which the subject is instituted and maintained, how it institutes and maintains itself, and how the norms that govern ethical principles must be understood as operating not only to guide conduct but to decide the question of who and what will be a human subject.

When Adorno tells us that only by becoming inhuman can we attain the possibility of becoming human, he underscores the disorientation at the heart of moral deliberation, the fact that the "I" who seeks to chart its course has not made the map it reads, does not have all the language it needs to read the map, and sometimes cannot find the map itself. The "I" emerges as a deliberating subject only once the world has appeared as a countervailing picture, an externality to be known and negotiated at an epistemological distance. This means that something historical has happened to produce the very possibility of this divergence and, accordingly, of moral deliberation itself. It also means that our deliberations will not make sense unless we can come to some understanding of the conditions that make our deliberation possible in the first place.

Whereas, for Adorno, there is always a bifurcation, a division that produces this possibility of an epistemological and ethical encounter with alterity, for Foucault, a given ontological regime sets a limit within which we remain constrained by binary thinking. For Adorno, Kant represents the culture of abstract reason, which is bifurcated from the consequences of its action; for Foucault, Kant heralds the possibility of critique by asking what conditions what I may know and how I may act. For Adorno, Kant offers a restricted conception of the human that forecloses from its very definition its error and its consequentiality. For Foucault, Kant's abstraction is a far cry from the "care for the self," but insofar as Kant insists that there are limits to our knowing, he seems to concede that a certain blindness and error afflict the project of knowledge from the start. Although Adorno faults Kant for not recognizing error as constitutive of the human and Foucault lauds him for apprehending precisely that, they both concur on the necessity of conceiving the human in its fallibility. If we are to act ethically, for either Adorno or Foucault, we must avow error as constitutive of who we are. This does not mean that we are only error, or that all we say is errant and wrong. But it does mean that what conditions our doing is a constitutive limit, for which we cannot give a full account, and this condition is, paradoxically, the basis of our accountability.

Foucault's Critical Account of Himself

> Do not ask who I am and do not ask me to remain the same. More than one person, doubtless like me, writes in order to have no face.
>
> —Michel Foucault, "What Is an Author?"

In "How Much Does It Cost for Reason to Tell the Truth,"[9] Foucault is asked to give an account of himself. His answer is not an easy one. He begins again and again, pointing to different influences but offering no causal explanation for why he came to think and act as he does. At the outset of the interview, he tries to understand the political implications of his own theory. He is clear that politics does not follow directly from theory. He notes, for instance, that there was an alliance between linguistic formalism and antiauthoritarian politics, but he does not say that the one leads to the other. The account he gives is not one that identifies causes and elaborates consequences. It is important to understand that this is a conversation and he is reacting to the presuppositions of his interlocutor, articulating his position in the context of that reaction. In a sense, the account he gives of himself is an account given to this person with these questions. The account cannot be understood outside the interlocutory scene in which it takes place. Is he telling the truth about himself, or is he responding to the demands that his interlocutor imposes upon him? How are we to engage his own practice of truth-telling in light of the theory of truth-telling that he devises in his later years?

In the last years of his life, Foucault returned to the question of confession,[10] reversing his earlier critique in the first volume of the *History of Sexuality*, where he indicts confession as a forcible extraction of sexual truth, a practice in the service of a regulatory power that produces the subject as one who is obligated to tell the truth about his or her desire. In the consideration of the practice of confession that he conducted in the early 1980s, he rewrote his earlier position, finding that confession compels a "manifestation" of the self that does not have to correspond to some putative inner truth, and whose constitutive appearance is *not* to be construed as mere illusion. On the contrary, in his lectures on Tertullian and Cassian Foucault reads confession as an act of speech in which the subject "publishes himself," gives himself in words, engages in an extended act of self-verbalization—*exomologesis*—as a way of making the self appear for another. Confession in this context presupposes that the self must appear in order to constitute itself and that it can constitute itself only within a given scene of address, within a certain socially constituted relation. Confession becomes the verbal and bodily scene of its self-demonstration. It speaks itself, but in the speaking it becomes what it is. In this context, then, self-examination is a practice of externalizing or publicizing oneself and, hence, at a distance from theories, including that of the early Foucault, that would assimilate confession to the violence of self-scrutiny and the forcible imposition of a regulatory discourse. Moreover, confession does not return a self to an equilibrium it has lost; it reconstitutes the soul on the basis of the act of confession itself. The sinner does not have to give an account that corresponds to events but only make himself manifest as a sinner. Thus a certain performative production of the subject within established public conventions is required of the confessing subject and constitutes the aim of confession itself.

Just as Foucault claims "the genealogy of the modern self . . . is one of the possible ways to get rid of a traditional philosophy of the subject" (H, 169), so he turns to confession to show how the subject must relinquish itself in and through the manifestation of the self it makes. In this sense, the manifestation of the self dissolves its inwardness and reconstitutes it in its externality. This dialectical inversion is worthy of Adorno and no doubt bears Hegelian resonances. Foucault writes about a specific confession in which an individual confesses to a theft, remarking that "the decisive element is not that the master knows the truth. It is not even that the young monk reveals his act and restores the object of his theft. It is the confession, the verbal act of confession, which comes last and which makes appear, in a certain sense, by its own mechanics, the truth, the reality of what has happened. The verbal act of confession is the proof, is the manifestation, of truth"(H, 178). In a sense, the theft is not avowed as a theft and is not socially constituted as a fact until it becomes manifest through the act of confession. Later in the same lecture, Foucault explains that the person who confesses must substitute the manifestation for the inward self. In this sense, manifestation does not "express" a self but takes its place, and it accomplishes that substitution through an inversion of the particular self into an outward appearance. Foucault concludes that we have to understand manifestation itself as an act of sacrifice, one that constitutes a change in life that follows the formula: "you will become the subject of a manifestation of truth when and only when you disappear or you destroy yourself as a real body and a real existence"(H, 179).

In the context of this model of confession, self-examination does not consist in self-beratement or, indeed, the internalization of regulatory norms but becomes a way of giving oneself over to a publicized mode of appearance. Even there, however, a preconstituted self is not revealed; instead, the very practice of self-constitution is performed. Indeed, a mode of reflexivity is stylized and maintained as a social and ethical practice. Thus Foucault moves the consideration of ethics beyond the problem of bad conscience, suggesting that neither the Freudian nor the Nietzschean account of the formation of conscience suffices for a conception of ethics. Moreover, he insists that the relation to the self is a social and public relation, one that is inevitably sustained in the context of norms that regulate reflexive relations: How might and must one appear? And what relation to oneself ought one manifest?

The consequences for a contemporary rethinking of the subject are not far afield. If I ask "Who might I be *for myself?*" I must also ask "What place is there for an 'I' in the discursive regime in which I live?" and "What modes of attending to the self have been established as the ones in which I might engage?" I am not bound to established forms of subject formation or, indeed, to established conventions for relating to myself, but I am bound to the sociality of any of those possible relations. I may risk intelligibility and defy convention, but then I am acting within or on a socio-historical horizon, attempting to rupture or transform it. But I become this self only through an ec-static movement, one that moves me outside of myself into a sphere in which I am dispossessed of myself and constituted as a subject at the same time.

In "How Much Does It Cost for Reason to Tell the Truth?" Foucault asks about the specifically modern ways in which the subject has come into question and relates his own process of arriving at the question of the subject. He realizes that no existing theory can accommodate the way he wants to pose the question. It is not that no existing theory has an answer to the question, though they doubtless do not. Rather, what matters is that no existing theory can provide terms to formulate the question he wants to pose.

Here is Foucault's question: "Can a transhistorical subject of a phenomenological kind be accounted for by a history of reason?" (HM, 238). Implicit in this question is the notion that something called "a transhistorical subject" can be accounted for. This is already to refuse the thesis of phenomenology, which is, in effect, that the transhistorical subject *accounts for* all experience and knowledge, that it is the ground of knowing. By asking what accounts for this "ground," Foucault implicitly argues that this ground is no ground, but comes to appear as a ground only after a certain historical process has taken place.

But he also makes another claim, one that engages historicism in a new way. He asks whether there is a history of reason that might account for the emergence of a transhistorical subject. In this sense, he is both suggesting that there is something called a history of reason and rejecting the claim of reason to be outside of history, to not have particular historical forms. Can there be a history of reason in Foucault's sense within phenomenology? (To his credit, Husserl moves in that direction in his *Crisis of the European Sciences*, a text that Foucault does not consider here.)

When Foucault claims that there is a history of the subject and a history of reason, he is also arguing that the history of reason cannot be derived from the subject. But he is maintaining that certain formations of the subject might be accounted for through the history of reason. The fact that the subject *has* a history disqualifies the subject from being the founding act by which the history of reason comes into being. But the history that the subject has is one in which reason has taken certain forms, in which rationality has been established and instituted with certain conditions and limits. So when, for instance, Foucault claims that a subject can recognize itself, and others, only within a specific regime of truth,[11] he is indexing one of these forms of rationality. We can see that only within certain forms of rationality can the subject, in a certain way, *be*. When he asks, then, how a transhistorical subject comes to be, he is implicitly refuting the possibility of a transhistorical subject, since the question exposes the subject as historically and variably made. But he is also honoring the notion, since such a concept comes to be, and to lay its claim upon us, precisely because it comes to make sense within a historically established mode of rationality, one that he here associates with phenomenology.

The interviewer wants to know whether the turn to Nietzsche was a sign of Foucault's dissatisfaction with phenomenology—whether, in particular, Nietzsche offered "the founding act of the subject a check [*pour couper court à l'acte fondateur du sujet*]" (HM, 239). And whether there was, during that time, a desire to articulate a theory of the subject that would not give it grand and overwhelming powers to found its own experience but that would understand that the subject comes always with limitations, is always made in part from something else that is not itself—a history, an unconscious, a set of structures, the history of reason—which gives the lie to its self-grounding pretensions.

Interestingly, when Foucault tries to give an account of why he read Nietzsche and says that he does not know, he is showing us, by his very confession of ignorance, that the subject cannot fully furnish the grounds for its own emergence. The account he gives of himself reveals that he does not know all the reasons that operated on him, in him, during that time. In trying to answer why he read him, he explains that others were reading him—Bataille and Blanchot. But he does not say why that supplies a reason—that is, that the reason he reads is that he needs to keep up, or because he was influenced. He read the one because of the others, but we do not know what kind of account this is. What was it that he read in the one that compelled him to turn to the other?

He is giving an account of himself, and he is explaining how he, and others, moved away from a phenomenology invested in "a kind of founding subject [*une sorte d'acte fondateur*]" (SP, 441), a subject who endows meaning through its acts of consciousness. Thus he is giving an account of himself as someone who is, quite clearly, not a founding subject but rather a subject with a history, one who is therefore disqualified from constituting the founding act by which the history of reason emerges. In giving this account of himself, he shows us the limits of the phenomenological conception of the subject.

Here, as elsewhere, the question that Foucault poses exposes the limits of our conventional ways of accounting for the subject. He maintains, for instance, that in the nineteenth century the question "What is Enlightenment?" emerges after the history of reason establishes the grounds for autonomy. This in turn raises a different question: "what history means to reason and which value the domination of reason must be accorded in the modern world" (SP, 438).

So the very question "What is Enlightenment?" introduces "an unsettling question" into the realm of reason, even though it was meant to return us to the centrality of reason and its critical function, to autonomy and its foundational status. A first and inadequate form of this unsettling question takes place when scholars asked, as they did, "What is the history of science?" For science to admit a history was a scandalous claim for those who claimed that science, in its rationality, had a truth that is transhistorical. In Germany the history of reason, a notion perhaps introduced in its modern form through the question of the history of science, turned to the history of forms of rationality. At this juncture Foucault asserts his alliance with the Frankfurt School, with some regret at the belatedness of the encounter: "If I had known the Frankfurt School at the right time, I would have been spared a lot of work. There are many stupidities that I would not have spoken and many detours that I would not have tried to follow down my own merry path since the way had already been opened by the Frankfurt School" (SP, 439).

All the same, he objects to what he calls the form of blackmail (*chantage*) that seeks to assimilate all criticism of reason to a negation of reason itself or threatens to castigate the critique as a form of irrationalism. Every regime of truth has recourse to this blackmail, which means that the blackmail belongs to no particular regime, indeed, may work in any number of regimes. This means that the very operation of the blackmail belies the thesis for which the blackmail is devised. The thesis is that there is a single regime, but the repeatability of the thesis in relation to different regimes establishes their plurality and exposes the blackmail as seeking to compel the recognition of a single regime of truth, which, in its repeatability, is shown not to be single at all.

Thus Foucault writes, "One has often tried to blackmail all criticism of reason and every critical test of rationality so that one either recognizes reason or casts it into irrationalism" (HM, 242). He is also loathe to accept the notion that reason is simply divided, although its division has, even for Adorno, supplied the basis for critique (HM, 243). The interviewer tries to describe this possibility of reflexivity as conditioned by a distinction between technical and practical (or moral) reason.

In a way, one can see Foucault's difference from Adorno and Habermas alike when he refuses the notion of a single bifurcation of reason, rejecting the view that there is a singular reason that simply has two different faces, as it were. This conception of a bifurcated reason emerges as part of the history of reason, proper to a specific mode of rationality. In his view, there is a difference between giving an account of how reason became technical and the ways in which men, life, and the self became objects of a certain number of *technai*. The answer to the former question cannot supply the answer to the latter. In this sense, there is a distinction between the history of reason (modes of rationality) and the history of subjectivation, for any adequate concept of rationality has to account for the kinds of subjects it facilitates and produces.

To say that reason undergoes a bifurcation is to assume that reason was once intact and whole prior to this self-division and that there is a founding act or a certain historical "moment" that mobilizes reason and its bifurcation. But why should we make that assumption? Do we need recourse to an original or, indeed, an ideal form of reason to begin to give an account of the history of reason? If we are interested in analyzing forms of rationality, then it would seem that we are obligated only to take the historical occurrence of rationality in its specificity, "without being able to designate a moment in which reason would have lost its basic design or changed from rationalism to irrationalism"(HM, 244).

There is no rationality that is the exemplary form of reason itself. As a result, we cannot talk about a golden day in which there was reason and then a set of events or historical shifts that plunged us into irrationalism. Foucault remarks that this is a second model from which he tried to free himself, but it seems intimately linked to the first. "I don't see how one can say that the forms of rationality . . . break apart and disperse. I simply see multiple transformations—but why should one call that the demise [*effondrement*] of reason?" (HM, 251).

Foucault focuses not only on forms of rationality but on how the human subject applies such forms to himself, thus opening up the questions of a certain reflexivity of the subject, the particular form that reflexivity takes, and how it is enabled by the operation of a historically specific mode of rationality.

The way he poses the question is telling: "How does it come to be that the human subject makes himself into an object of possible knowledge, through which forms of rationality, through which historical conditions, and, finally, *at what price?*" (SP, 442, my emphasis). This way of putting the question enacts his methodology: There will be a reflexive action of a subject, and this action will be occasioned by the very rationality to which it attempts to conform or, at least, with which it negotiates. This form of rationality will foreclose others, so that one will become knowable to oneself only within the terms of a given rationality, historically conditioned, leaving open and unaddressed what other ways there may have been, or may well yet be, in the course of history.

We can see two separate developments here in Foucault's work. First, the notion of the subject at work here, specifically, the emergence of a reflexive subject, is distinctly different from the views set forth in the first volume of *The History of Sexuality*. Second, Foucault alters the theory of discursive construction. The subject is no simple effect or function of a prior form of rationality, but neither does reflexivity assume a single structure. Moreover, when the subject becomes an object for itself, it also misses something of itself; this occlusion is constitutive of the process of reflexivity.

For a brief moment, Foucault here shares a thesis with psychoanalysis. Something is sacrificed, lost, or at least spent or given up at the moment in which the subject makes himself into an object of possible knowledge. He cannot "know" what is lost through some cognitive means, but he can open up the question of what is lost by exercising the *critical* function of thought. Thus, Foucault poses his question: "How much does it cost the subject to be able to tell the truth about itself?" In a sense, this question is a leap from what comes before, but let us consider how it comes about. The human subject applies forms of rationality to itself, but this self-application comes at a price. What is the nature of this self-application such that it exacts something from the subject? What is there to be exacted?

What is there to be spent? He will not say that there is a demise of reason here, but he is also taking his distance from a self-satisfied form of constructivism. He is making clear that we are not simply the effects of discourses, but that any discourse, any regime of intelligibility, constitutes us *at a cost*. Our capacity to reflect upon ourselves, to tell the truth about ourselves, is correspondingly limited by what the discourse, the regime, cannot allow into speakability.

As a result, when Foucault starts making clear and determined pronouncements about himself, what he has always thought, and who he finally is, we have every reason to be cautious. Here is one such grand proclamation: "My problem is the relationship of self to self and that of saying the truth" (HM, 248). Although earlier we heard much from him on the matter of power, sexuality, bodies, and desire, he tells us now, as if in a moment of self-revision that retroactively extends over his entire past: "My problem never ceased to be always the truth, speaking truth [*le dire vrai*], *wahr-sagen*—that is, the speaking of truth—and the relationship [*le rapport*] between speaking truth and the forms of reflexivity, the reflexivity of self on self [*le soi sur soi*]" (SP, 445). This seems to mean that the forms of rationality by which we make ourselves intelligible, by which we know ourselves and offer ourselves to others, are established historically, and at a price. If they become naturalized, taken for granted, considered as foundational and required, if they become the terms by which we do and must live, then our very living depends upon a denial of their historicity, a disavowal of the price we pay.

In Foucault, it seems, there is a price for telling the truth about oneself, precisely because what constitutes the truth will be framed by norms and by specific modes of rationality that emerge historically and are, in that sense, contingent. Insofar as we do tell the truth, we conform to a criterion of truth, and we accept that criterion as binding upon us. To accept that criterion as binding is to assume as primary or unquestionable the form of rationality within which one lives. So telling the truth about oneself comes at a price, and the price of that telling is the suspension of a critical relation to the truth regime in which one lives. This means that when Foucault tells us the truth about himself, namely, that telling the truth was always his concern, that he always cared about the reflexivity of the self, we have to ask whether he has, for the moment, suspended a critical capacity in order to conform to a truth-telling requirement of the subject. When he claims that he has always had at the forefront of his mind the problem of truth-telling itself, he may or may not be telling the truth. After all, he is conceding that telling the truth is a kind of problem, and that the problem has been central to his thinking. We cannot settle the question of whether he is telling us the truth without denying the problem he would have us see.

This kind of declaration becomes more unsettling when he goes on to say that this turn to truth, and to reflexivity, is also more important than his considerations of power. On the one hand, he is establishing a historical continuity for himself. On the other hand, he tells us quite clearly that the description of today "must be formulated in a kind of virtual break" (HM, 252). This break is said to open freedom, to inaugurate a possible transformation, to interrogate the conditioning limits of one's time, and to risk the self at that limit. "Breaking" appears to be a figure for the act of critique that calls into question the fixity of a given mode of rationality, but here Foucault starts to narrate himself in a way that will make it appear that he has been self-identical through time.

When he considers the forms of rationality that provide the means by which subjectivation occurs, he writes, "these forms of rationality that are put to work in processes of domination merit being analyzed for themselves . . . these forms of rationality are not strangers to other forms of power at work, for example, in recognition [*connaissance*] or technology [*la technique*]" (SP, 449). So these forms of rationality are not strangers to one another, but we do not know in precisely what relation to each other they stand. Earlier he claims that rationality produces subjectivation by regulating the means by which recognition can occur. Here he refers to *connaissance* and not *reconnaissance*, so it is unclear whether we are entitled to understand the former in terms of the latter. Perhaps this can be clarified by the passage from "The Subject and Power" in which he refers to the "form of power . . . which categorizes, marks [a subject] by his own individuality, attaches him to his own identity, imposes a law of truth on him which he must recognize and which others have to recognize in him. It is a form of power which makes individuals subjects."[12] In the first chapter of *The Use of Pleasure*, he links the effectivity of discursive practices to subjectivating norms through the category of *recognition*. There he proposes to "analyze the practices by which individuals were led to focus their attention on themselves, to decipher, recognize, and acknowledge themselves as subjects of desire, bringing into play between themselves and themselves a certain relationship that allows them to discover, in desire, the truth of their being, be it natural or fallen"(*UP*, 5).

In each of these instances, forms of rationality are tied to discursive practices or to the forms of subjectivation Foucault notes elsewhere. If the forms of rationality that concern him in 1983 are not alien to other forms of power, such as recognition, then Foucault concedes that recognition is a form of power, even as he maintains that it is distinct from the forms of rationality—understood as part of the history of reason—that he describes here. In the midst of trying to understand how these various forms of power interrelate, he cautions us against devising a single theory of power that would identify their common denominator in any satisfying way. He gives an account of his own theoretical practice when, for instance, he claims, in a simple declarative mode: "I create no theory of power [*Je ne fait pas une théorie du pouvoir*]" or "I am no theoretician of power. The question of power in itself doesn't interest me [*Je ne suis pas donc aucunement un théoricien du pouvoir. À la limite, je dirais que le pouvoir ne m'interesse pas comme une question autonome*]" (HM, 254). In a sense, he is right, if by a "theory" of power one means a full analytic explanation of power apart from its concrete operations as if it were autonomous. He had told us that for some time; he writes, for instance, in "The Subject and Power" that "I would say that to begin the analysis with a 'how' is to suggest that power as such does not exist."[13] On several occasions, he counseled that we must be "nominalists" about power. We cannot ask the standard theoretical question, "What is power?" We can ask only, "How does power work, or what form does power take in this or that exercise, and what does it do?"

What allows Foucault to tell the truth about himself here, but also constrains his speech in the telling? About insanity Foucault writes, "The subject was able to tell the truth about his insanity, because the structures of the Other allowed him to. That was possible as a result of a specific kind of dominance, which some persons exerted over others"(HM, 254). What price is paid here, when the account of himself he is able to give is indebted to being dominated by others and by their discourse? Can the truth he tells about himself tell the truth about dominance, or does the ethical sphere, when considered separately from the operation of power, always engage in a disavowal of power and, in this sense, in a form of concealment? One way to read Foucault's insistence that now he is interested in truth-telling, that he was always interested in truth-telling, is to see that one asks the question of power only because of the demand to tell the truth about oneself. Who is asking this of me? What do they expect? In what language will my answer satisfy? What are the consequences of telling and of not telling the truth about myself to this interlocutor?

If the question of power and the demand to tell the truth about oneself are linked, then the need to give an account of oneself necessitates the turn to power, so that we might say that the ethical demand gives rise to the political account, and that ethics undermines its own credibility when it does not become critique. Thus Foucault embeds truth-telling within the account of how power works: "If I 'tell the truth' about myself, I constitute myself as subject by a certain number of relationships of power, which weigh upon me and which I lay upon others" (HM, 254).

Here he puts "tell the truth" in quotation marks, calling into question whether telling the truth is as truthful an enterprise as it seems. If power relations weigh upon me as I tell the truth and if, in telling the truth, I am bringing the weight of power to bear upon others, then I am not simply communicating the truth when I am telling the truth. I am also putting power to work in discourse, using it, distributing it, becoming the site for its relay and replication. I am speaking, and my speech conveys what I take to be true. But my speaking is also a kind of doing, an action that takes place within the field of power and that also constitutes an act of power.

In Foucault's 1983 lectures at Berkeley, he examined the practice of telling the truth about oneself in relation to the classical Greek concept of *parrhesia*, speaking out or speaking the truth in public.[14] These lectures, published in English and German,[15] revisit the practice of giving an account of oneself in Plato's dialogues and in Seneca's essay "On Anger." In some ways, they give a final rendition of the themes we have been considering here. The self's reflexivity is incited by an other, so that one person's discourse leads another person into self-reflection. The self does not simply begin to examine itself through the forms of rationality at hand. Those forms of rationality are delivered through discourse, in the form of an address, and they arrive as an incitement, a form of seduction, an imposition or demand from outside to which one yields.

My students have always objected to the passivity of the Socratic interlocutor in Plato's dialogues. Foucault gives us a way to revisit the question of that passivity, for persuasion is not possible without yielding to another's words. Indeed, there is no way of forgiving another or being forgiven without the possibility of yielding to another's words. Thus Foucault writes of a yielding that animates speech in Plato's dialogue *The Laches*: "the listener is led by the Socratic *logos* into 'giving an account'—*didonai logon*—of himself, of the manner in which he now spends his days, and of the kind of life he has led hitherto" (Plato, *Laches*, 187e–188c; *FS*, 96). The listener is being led, and so yielding to another's lead. This passivity becomes the condition of a certain practice of giving an account of oneself, suggesting that one can become accountable only through yielding to another's word, another's demand. This is, according to Foucault, "a practice where the one who is being led by Socrates' discourse must give an autobiographical account of his life, or a confession of his faults" (*FS*, 96). Foucault is quick to point out that this account of oneself is not the same as self-blame:

> what is involved is not a confessional autobiography. In Plato's or Xenophon's portrayals of him, we never see Socrates requiring an examination of conscience or a confession of sins. Here, giving an account of your life, your *bios*, is also not to give a narrative of the historical events that have taken place in your life, but rather to demonstrate whether you are able to show that there is a relation between the rational discourse, the *logos*, you are able to use, and the way that you live. Socrates is inquiring into the way that *logos* gives form to a person's style of life. (*FS*, 97)

If one is speaking in giving an account of oneself, then one is also exhibiting, in the very speech that one uses, the logos by which one lives. The point is not only to bring speech into accord with action, although this is the emphasis that Foucault provides; it is also to acknowledge that speaking is already a kind of doing, a form of action, one that is already a moral practice and a way of life. Moreover, it presupposes a social exchange. In considering the Cynics, Foucault rehearses the struggle between Alexander and Diogenes in a text by Dio Chrysostom in the second century A.D. in which Diogenes is said to "expose himself to Alexander's power from the beginning to the end of the Discourse. And the main effect of this parrhesiastic struggle with power is not to bring the interlocutor to a new truth, or to a new level of self-awareness; it is to lead the interlocutor to *internalize* this parrhesiastic struggle—to fight within himself against his own faults, and to be with himself in the same way that Diogenes was with him" (*FS*, 133).

One might be tempted to find here a kind of transferential relation *avant la lettre*, one that might resituate psychoanalysis as part of the history of the "care of the self." Although for the most part Foucault either identifies psychoanalysis with the repressive hypothesis (the anteriority of desire to the law or the production of desire as a consequence of law) or sees it as an instrument of the inward mutilations of "conscience," we can discern some similarities between the two positions that would suggest another direction for inquiry into the self. After all, Foucault moves in his late lectures to a consideration of the passivity of reception as well as the transitivity of instruction. Both of these, along with his remarks about internalizing the other, lay the groundwork for a possible dialogue between Foucault and psychoanalysis.

Foucault indicates as much when he writes, in *Hermeneutics of the Subject*, that analytic knowledge of the self might properly belong to the tradition of spiritual self-care whose early versions he is tracing in late antiquity. He credits Lacan with having been the only one since Freud to recenter the question of psychoanalysis on the question of the relation between the subject and truth (*HDS*, 31). In this context, he acknowledges that the question he has been posing, "How much does it cost a subject to tell the truth?" traverses antiquity and psychoanalysis alike: "the question of the price that the subject has paid to speak the truth, and the question of the effect on the subject to do what he has said" (ibid.). This question resurfaces, Foucault maintains, when one finds at "the very interior of psychoanalysis the resurgence of the oldest tradition, the oldest interrogation, this oldest disquietude that belongs to this injunction to take 'care of the self' which is the most general form of spirituality" (ibid.).

Foucault remarks upon these early relations of the self to itself, to the truth of what it speaks, and to the other in order to show, time and again, its distance from the modern permutation of the confessional, one that he had earlier associated with the disciplinary effects of psychiatry and psychoanalysis. When he refers to Seneca's form of self-examination, he points out that "he discloses no secret faults, no shameful desires" (*FS* 152). And at the end of his discussion of Epictetus, he distinguishes clearly between a moralized relation to the self and the moral practice of self-care. He writes:

> These exercises are part of what we would call an "aesthetics of the self." For one does not have to take up a position as that of a judge pronouncing a verdict. One can comport oneself towards oneself in the role of a technician, of a craftsman, of an artist, who from time to time stops working, examines what he is doing, reminds himself of the rules of the art, and compares these rules with what he has achieved so far. (*FS* 166)

Of course, Foucault's subject is deliberative and intentional in these descriptions, but his analysis of the passions, including "anger," is an effort to come to grips with what drives a person at a level that is recalcitrant to self-reflection and self-making. When he refers to exercises in which someone has to examine the truth about himself in the form of an address to another, he is clear that "the expression 'examination of conscience' as a blanket term meant to characterize all these different exercises misleads and oversimplifies" (*FS*, 144–45). In these lectures from the 1980s, self-examination takes place in the form of an address to another, after having been addressed (pedagogically) by another. However, the relation to the other is not as constitutive or disruptive as it is in Levinas or Laplanche. In Foucault, we will not find an interrogation of passions of the soul that bear an irreversible imprint of the other on the self and that, by definition, disrupt any effort to establish self-mastery. Self-mastery takes place in an address to an other or in an exposition before the other, contextualized and facilitated by a pedagogical relationship.

We find in Foucault an understanding that reflexivity, self-care, and self-mastery are all open-ended and unsatisfiable efforts to "return" to a self from the situation of being foreign to oneself. Here Foucault's difference from both Laplanche and Levinas is obvious. For Levinas, "self-recurrence" is infinite, can never be accomplished, and takes place at an an-archic level, permanently prior to conscious reflection. For Laplanche, the constitutive foreignness that gives rise to drives is an insuperable condition of the "I" and its affects. The subject of "self-care" in Foucault works on the self as a kind of material, but we might ask about the recalcitrance and obduracy of this material. Here Foucault and psychoanalysis part ways. For Foucault, this is an open-ended task, one that can have no final form. He thus disputes notions of progress or rational development that would take hold of the reflexive relation and guide it toward a clear conclusion. The self is formed in history, but the history of the individual self, the history of individuation, is not given: There is no infancy here, no primacy of the imprint of the Other, no account of the specific relationality by which an infant self develops its separateness, and at what price. Foucault understands that, in considering the Socratic, Stoic, Cynical, and materialist views of self-care, he is at a remove from modern notions of reflexivity. But this contrast is crucial to the "critical" operation of his text, since modern conceptions of the self are neither true nor inevitable, but have been made through a complex history of indebtedness and disavowal in relation to these, and other, earlier formations of the self.

In *Hermeneutics of the Subject*, he considers the Delphic oracle that guides Socrates—"Know thyself!"—and concludes that one can know oneself only if the subject has a relation to truth. If truth is to be found as logos, as a principle and structure of language and, specifically, as the demonstrative properties of speech, then the very possibility of knowing oneself depends on being able to elaborate the subject's relation to truth and to speech. Is the subject capable of speaking the truth of itself? He realizes that for the views of the self that he considers from Greek and Roman antiquity the presumption that having access to truth is *not* fundamentally at odds with the "being of the subject" (*HDS*, 20). Foucault marks a clear historical difference from the modern situation, in which truth neither defines nor saves the subject: this former "point of illumination, this point of accomplishment, the moment of the transfiguration of the subject by virtue of the 'effect of a return' of a truth that he knows about himself, and which transports, traverses, transfigures his being, all of this is no longer possible" (ibid.). Neither reward nor accomplishment, knowledge, under modern conditions, moves along an "indefinite path." Although we are capable of pursuing and speaking what we take to be the truth, it does not finally return to us to reveal, restore, or consecrate some primary truth of who we are, to reward us for our labor or our sacrifice. In the modern age, Foucault writes, we are indeed capable of having a relation to truth: "the subject is capable of truth, such as it is, but the truth is not capable of saving the subject" (ibid.).

This ironic conclusion does not preclude the possibility that some change may happen along the way. After all, when one gives an account of oneself one is not merely relaying information through an indifferent medium. The account is an act—situated within a larger practice of acts—that one performs for, to, even *on* an other, an allocutory deed, an acting for, and in the face of, the other and sometimes by virtue of the language provided by the other. This account does not have as its goal the establishment of a definitive narrative but constitutes a linguistic and social occasion for self-transformation. Considered pedagogically, it constitutes part of what Socrates exemplified about *parrhesia* as courageous speaking in a critical spirit in "The Apology." In Foucault's terms, "the target of this new *parrhesia* is not to persuade the Assembly, but to convince someone that he must take care of himself and of others; and this means that he must *change his life*" (*FS*, 106).

How one speaks and how one lives are not separate enterprises, even though, as Foucault reminds us, discourse is not life. In speaking to another, and at another's request, about how one has lived, one is responding to a request, and one is attempting to establish or re-establish a certain bond, to honor the fact that one has been addressed from elsewhere. So, when it is a matter of giving an account of oneself, is one ever *only* speaking, or ever *only* doing? Foucault refers to "the *bios-logos* relation [that is] disclosed when the interlocutor gives an account of his life, and its harmony tested by contact with Socrates" (*FS*, 101). Giving an account is thus also a kind of showing of oneself, a showing for the purpose of testing whether the account seems right, whether it is understandable by the other, who "receives" the account through one set of norms or another.

I have a relation to myself, but I have it in the context of an address to an other. So the relation is disclosed, but it is also, to borrow from Foucault's work on confession, *published*, brought into the realm of appearance, constituted as a social manifestation. Re-linking truth-telling to the problem of power, he remarks that in the fifth century B.C. philosophical problems emerge in relation to questions about the allocation of power: Who is able to tell the truth, about what, with what consequences, and with what relation to power? Although truth-telling is compelled to proceed according to rules of validity, Foucault also makes clear that there are conditions—I would call them rhetorical—that make truth-telling possible and that must be interrogated. In this sense, the problematization of truth must take into account "the importance of telling the truth, knowing who is able to tell the truth, and knowing why we should tell the truth." These questions, which concern the limits, the conditions, and the consequences of truth-telling as such, contain, in his words, "the roots of what we could call the 'critical' tradition in the West" (*FS*, 170).

These questions constitute the roots of "what we could call the 'critical' tradition," suggesting, perhaps, that we do not regularly include this kind of inquiry as part of the critical tradition, but clearly should. Foucault allies himself with the critical tradition, but will anyone extend him a welcoming hand? In his insistence on conditions of power in which the problem of truth-telling emerges, Foucault is not so far from Adorno, for whom moral deliberation itself is a consequence of a certain historical condition, in which the subject is produced at a distance from the instrumentally conceived objective world. When I tell the truth about myself, I consult not only my "self," but the way in which that self is produced and producible, the position from which the demand to tell the truth proceeds, the effects that telling the truth will have in consequence, as well as the price that must be paid.

For each of these thinkers in different ways, a price must be paid. To tell the truth about oneself involves us in quarrels about the formation of the self and the social status of truth. Our narratives come up against an impasse when the conditions of possibility for speaking the truth cannot fully be thematized, where what we speak relies upon a formative history, a sociality, and a corporeality that cannot easily, if at all, be reconstructed in narrative. Paradoxically, I become dispossessed in the telling, and in that dispossession an ethical claim takes hold, since no "I" belongs to itself. From the outset, it comes into being through an address I can neither recall nor recuperate, and when I act, I act in a world whose structure is in large part not of my making—which is not to say that there is no making and no acting that is mine. There surely is. It means only that the "I," its suffering and acting, telling and showing, take place within a crucible of social relations, variously established and iterable, some of which are irrecoverable, some of which impinge upon, condition, and limit our intelligibility within the present. And when we do act and speak, we not only disclose ourselves but act on the schemes of intelligibility that govern who will be a speaking being, subjecting them to rupture or revision, consolidating their norms, or contesting their hegemony.

For Adorno, the question of what I ought to do is implicated in a social analysis of the world in which my doing takes shape and has effects. In his view, an ethics of responsibility not only takes into account "the end and the intention" of my action, but "the resultant shaping of the world" (*PMP*, 172). For him, the question of how to live a good life in a bad life, how to persist subjectively in a good life when the world is poorly organized, is but a different way of claiming that moral worth cannot be considered apart from its conditions and consequences. In his words, "anything that we can call morality today merges into the question of the organization of the world. We might even say that the quest for the good life is the quest for the right form of politics, if indeed such a right form of politics lay within the realm of what can be achieved today" (*PMP*, 176).

In a sympathetic critique of Nietzsche, Adorno cautions against various misleading ways in which one might interpret the task of creating new values. He remarks that "in reality" the "lone individual" is "impotent" simply to "set up new norms and new commandments based on his own subjective whim," calling this task "arbitrary" and "adventitious" (*PMP*, 172). Slightly later in his lecture, he criticizes Nietzsche for not attending radically enough to changing the "conditions that determine human beings and make them and each of us who we are"(*PMP*, 174). Foucault in some ways takes over the job that Nietzsche left only partially completed. And though Foucault does not celebrate the 'lone individual' who simply makes up new norms, he would locate the practices of the subject as one site where those social conditions are worked and reworked.

If, according to Foucault, new modes of subjectivity become possible, this does not follow from the fact that there are individuals with especially creative capacities. Such modes of subjectivity are produced when the limiting conditions by which we are made prove to be malleable and replicable, when a certain self is risked in its intelligibility and recognizability in a bid to expose and account for the inhuman ways in which "the human" continues to be done and undone. Not every condition of the subject is open to revision, since the conditions of formation are not always recuperable and knowable, even as they live on, enigmatically, in the impulses that are our own. Whether as a deliberately reflexive attitude toward the self or as a mode of living what can never be fully known, the subject becomes a problem for moral philosophy precisely because it shows us how the human is constituted and deconstituted, the modes of its agentic self-making as well as its ways of living on. When we come up against the limits of any epistemological horizon and realize that the question is not simply whether I can or will *know* you, or whether I can be *known*, we are compelled to realize as well that "you" qualify in the scheme of the human within which I operate, and that no "I" can begin to tell its story without asking: "Who are you?" "Who speaks to me?" "To whom do I speak when I speak to you?" If this establishes the priority of rhetoric to ethics, that might be just as well. The mode of address conditions and structures the way in which moral questions emerge. The one who makes a claim on me, who asks me, as it were, who I am, what I have done, may well have a singularity and irreplaceability, but he also speaks in a language that is impersonal and that belongs to historically changing horizons of intelligibility. If Levinas has a point in saying that the Other is impressed upon us from the start, we concede, with Laplanche, that human life has a way of starting with infancy, then these primary impressions are bound up with the formation of the ego, the establishment of the unconscious, and the instigation of primary impulse in relation to an enigma, a foreignness, that is ours without ever belonging to us.

Similarly, Foucault and Adorno in different ways recall us to the deliberative dimensions of moral inquiry, the difficulty of being formed as a reflexive subject within a given social world. The self at issue is clearly "formed" within a set of social conventions that raise the question whether a good life can be conducted within a bad one, and whether we might, in recrafting ourselves with and for another, participate in the remaking of social conditions. Giving an account of oneself comes at a price not only because the "I" that I present cannot present many of the conditions of its own formation but because the "I" that yields to narration cannot comprise many dimensions of itself: the social parameters of address, the norms through which the "I" becomes intelligible, the non-narratable or even unspeakable dimensions of the unconscious that persist as an enabling foreignness at the heart of my desire.

What perhaps emerges most emphatically from the conjunction of these very disparate positions (Adorno, Foucault, Laplanche, Levinas, Nietzsche, Hegel) is that the response to the demand to give an account of oneself is a matter of fathoming at once the formation of the subject (self, ego, *moi*, first-person perspective) and its relation to responsibility. A subject who can never fully give an account of itself may well be a result of being related at non-narratable levels of existence to others in ways that have a supervenient ethical significance. If the "I" cannot effectively be disjoined from the impress of social life, then ethics will surely not only presuppose rhetoric (and the analysis of the mode of address) but social critique as well. The Nietzschean postulation of the self as a "cause" has a genealogy that must be understood as part of the reduction of ethical philosophy to the inward mutilations of conscience. Such a move not only severs the task of ethics from the matter of social life and the historically revisable grids of intelligibility within which any of us emerge, if we do, but it fails to understand the resource of primary and irreducible relations to others as a precondition of ethical responsiveness. One might rightly quarrel with the postulation of a preontological persecution by the Other in Levinas or offer an account that challenges the primacy of seduction in Laplanche. But either way, one must ask how the formation of the subject implies a framework for understanding ethical response and a theory of responsibility. If certain versions of self-preoccupied moral inquiry return us to a narcissism that is supported through socially enforced modes of individualism, and if that narcissism also leads to an ethical violence that knows no grace of self-acceptance or forgiveness, then it would seem obligatory, if not urgent, to return the question of responsibility to the question "How are we formed within social life, and at what cost?"

Perhaps most importantly, we must recognize that ethics requires us to risk ourselves precisely at moments of unknowingness, when what forms us diverges from what lies before us, when our willingness to become undone in relation to others constitutes our chance of becoming human. To be undone by another is a primary necessity, an anguish, to be sure, but also a chance—to be addressed, claimed, bound to what is not me, but also to be moved, to be prompted to act, to address myself elsewhere, and so to vacate the self-sufficient "I" as a kind of possession. If we speak and try to give an account from this place, we will not be irresponsible, or, if we are, we will surely be forgiven.

CHAPTER 1. AN ACCOUNT OF ONESELF

1. Theodor Adorno, *Problems of Moral Philosophy*, trans. Rodney Livingstone (Stanford: Stanford University Press, 2001), 16; *Probleme der Moralphilosophie* (Frankfurt am Main: Suhrkamp, 1997), 30. Hereafter cited as *PMP* in the text, with page numbers referring to the English translation.

2. Judith Butler, Ernesto Laclau, and Slavoj Žižek, *Contingency, Hegemony, Universality* (London: Verso, 2000).

3. For a brilliant and engaging analysis of the immersion and dispossession of the "I" in social conventions, as well as its implications for both lyric poetry and social solidarities, see Denise Riley, *Words of Selves: Identification, Solidarity, Irony* (Stanford: Stanford University Press, 2000).

4. Friedrich Nietzsche, *On the Genealogy of Morals*, trans. Walter Kaufmann (New York: Random House, 1969), 80; *Zur Genealogie der Moral*, in *Kritische Studienausgabe*, ed. Giorgio Colli and Mazzino Montinari (Berlin: de Gruyter, 1967–77) 5: 245–412. Hereafter cited in the text as *GM*, with page numbers referring to the English edition.

5. Judith Butler, *The Psychic Life of Power* (Stanford: Stanford University Press, 1997).

6. Michel Foucault, *The Use of Pleasure: The History of Sexuality, Volume Two* (New York: Random House, 1985); *Histoire de la sexualité 2: L'Usage des plaisirs* (Paris: Gallimard, 1984). Hereafter cited as *UP* in the text, with page numbers referring to the English translation.

7. See Judith Butler, "What Is Critique? On Foucault's Virtue," in *The Political*, ed. David Ingram (London: Basel Blackwell, 2002), 212–26.

8. Michel Foucault, "What Is Critique?" in *The Political*, ed. David Ingram, 191–211, here p. 194. This essay was originally a lecture given at the French Society of Philosophy on May 27, 1978; it was subsequently published in *Bulletin de la Société Française de la philosophie* 84, no. 2 (1990): 35–63.

9. Adriana Cavarero, *Relating Narratives: Storytelling and Selfhood*, trans. Paul A. Kottman (London: Routledge, 2000); *Tu che mi guardi, tu che mi racconti* (Milan: Giagiacomo Feltrinelli, 1997). It is interesting to compare Cavarero's text not only with Riley's *Words of Selves* but also with Paul Ricouer, *Oneself as Another*, trans. Kathleen Blamey (Chicago: University of Chicago Press, 1992); *Soi-même comme un autre* (Paris: Seuil, 1990). Ricouer, like Cavarero, makes a case both for the constitutive sociality of the self and for its capacity to present itself in narrative, though they proceed in very different ways. Riley focuses on lyric poetry and ordinary language use, suggesting a non-narrative problem of referentiality generated by the formal structure of linguistic conventions.

10. See Emmanuel Levinas, *Otherwise than Being, or beyond Essence*, trans. Alphonso Lingis (The Hague: Martinus Nijhoff, 1981); *Autrement qu'être ou au-dela de l'essence* (The Hague: Martinus Nijhoff, 1974). Hereafter cited in the text as *OB*, with page numbers referring to the English translation.

11. Foucault, "What Is Critique?" 192.

12. G. W. F. Hegel, *The Phenomenology of Spirit*, trans. A. V. Miller (Oxford: Oxford University Press, 1977), 111–12; *Werke in zwanzig Bänden*, vol. 3 (Frankfurt am Main: Suhrkamp, 1980).

13. See Nathan Rotenstreich, "On the Ecstatic Sources of the Concept of Alienation," in *Review of Metaphysics*, 1963; Jean-Luc Nancy, *Hegel: The Restlessness of the Negative*, trans. Jason Smith and Steven Miller (Minneapolis: University of Minnesota Press, 2002), in French, *Hegel: L'Inquiétude du négatif* (Paris: Hachette Littératures, 1997); Catherine Malabou, *L'Avenir de Hegel: Plasticité, temporalité, dialectique* (Paris: J. Vrin, 1996).

14. For a further reflection on this issue, see the final chapter, "Precarious Life," in my *Precarious Life: The Powers of Mourning and Violence* (London, Verso: 2004).

15. Foucault, "What Is Critique?" 191.

16. Hannah Arendt, *The Human Condition* (Chicago: University of Chicago Press, 1958), p. 183; cited partially in Cavarero, *Relating Narratives*, p. 20. Future references to Cavarero's book will appear as page numbers in the text.

17. Hegel, *Phenomenology of Spirit*, 66.

18. Michel Foucault, "The Politics of Discourse," in *The Foucault Effect: Studies in Governmentality*, ed. Graham Burchell, Colin Gordon, and Peter Miller (Chicago: University of Chicago Press, 1991), 70–72.

19. Thomas Keenan, *Fables of Responsibility: Aberrations and Predicaments in Ethics and Politics* (Stanford: Stanford University Press, 1997).

20. The narrative works as allegory, attempting to give a sequential account for that which cannot, finally, be grasped in sequential terms, for that which has a temporality or a spatiality that can be denied, displaced, or transmuted only when it assumes narrative form. Indeed, it may be that what I am perhaps boldly calling the referent here works as a constant threat to narrative authority even as it functions as the paradoxical condition for a narrative, a narrative that gives provisional and fictive sequence to that which necessarily eludes that construction. See Stephen Greenblatt, ed., *Allegory and Representation: Selected Papers from the English Institute, 1979–80* (Baltimore: The Johns Hopkins University Press, 1990).

21. Shoshana Felman, *The Scandal of the Speaking Body: Don Juan with J. L. Austin, or Seduction in Two Languages*, trans. Catherine Porter (Stanford: Stanford University Press, 2003).

CHAPTER 2. AGAINST ETHICAL VIOLENCE

1. For a consideration of transparency and illumination along these lines, see M. H. Abrams, *The Mirror and the Lamp: Romantic Theory and the Critical Tradition* (Oxford: Oxford University Press, 1953).

2. Jacques Lacan, *The Seminar of Jacques Lacan*, Book VII, *The Ethics of Psychoanalysis, 1959–1960*, ed., Jacques-Alain Miller, trans. Dennis Porter (New York: W. W. Norton, 1997), 321.

3. I consider this further in "The Desire to Live: Spinoza's *Ethics* under Pressure," in Victoria Kahn and Neil Saccamano, eds., *Passions and Politics* (Princeton: Princeton University Press, forthcoming).

4. Gilles Deleuze makes this point somewhat differently in his efforts to distinguish morality (which is concerned with judgment) from ethics. He writes, for instance: "Morality is the system of judgment. Of double judgment, you judge yourself and you are judged. Those who have the taste for morality are those who have the taste for judgment. Judging always implies an authority superior to Being, it always implies something superior to an ontology. It always implies one more than Being, the Good

which makes Being and which makes action, it is the Good superior to Being, it is the One. Value expresses this authority superior to Being. Therefore, values are the fundamental element of the system of judgment. Therefore, you are always referred to this authority superior to Being for judging. // In an ethics, it is completely different, you do not judge. In a certain manner, you say: whatever you do, you will only ever have what you deserve. Somebody says or does something, you do not relate it to values. You ask yourself how is that possible? How is this possible in an internal way? In other words, you relate the thing or the statement to the mode of existence that it implies, that it envelops in itself. How must it be in order to say that? Which manner of Being does this imply? You seek the enveloped modes of existence, and not the transcendent values. It is the operation of immanence" (Cours Vincennes, 12/21/1980, http://www .webdeleuze.com/php/texte.php?cle = 190&groupe = Spinoza&langue = 2).

5. See my "Beauvoir on Sade: Making Sexuality into an Ethic," in *Cambridge Companion to Simone de Beauvoir*, ed. Claudia Card (Cambridge: Cambridge University Press, 2004), 168–88.

6. Franz Kafka, *The Metamorphosis, The Penal Colony, and Other Stories*, trans. Willa and Edwin Muir (New York: Schocken, 1975), 49–63; Franz Kafka, *Die Erzählungen* (Frankfurt am Main: S. Fischer, 1998), 47–60.

7. I am grateful here to Barbara Johnson, who formulates the default structure of address in writing of Baudelaire, "the mother functions as a default setting for the I-you relationship in general" (*Mother Tongues: Sexuality, Trials, Motherhood, Translation* [Cambridge: Harvard University Press, 2003], 71).

8. See Shoshana Felman, *The Scandal of the Speaking Body: Don Juan with J. L. Austin, or Seduction in Two Languages*, trans. Catherine Porter (Stanford: Stanford University Press, 2003).

9. For an account of psychoanalysis and language that in general refuses passive constitution and privileges the "I" and its actions as the building blocks of a life story, see Roy Schafer, *A New Language for Psychoanalysis* (New Haven: Yale University Press, 1976), 22–56. For a concept of the relation to narrative structure in psychoanalysis that incorporates a notion of transference, see Peter Brooks, *Psychoanalysis and Story-telling* (Oxford: Basil Blackwell, 1994).

10. See Denise Riley, *Impersonal Passion: Language as Affect* (Durham, N.C.: Duke University Press, 2005). See also Thomas Keenan, *Fables of Responsibility: Aberrations and Predicaments in Ethics and Politics* (Stanford: Stanford University Press, 1997), 175–92. For an excellent discussion of feminist autobiographical narrative and its contestation of truth-telling standards, see Leigh Gilmore, *The Limits of Autobiography: Trauma and Testimony* (Ithaca, N.Y.: Cornell University Press, 2001).

11. Jean Laplanche, *Essays on Otherness*, ed. John Fletcher (London: Routledge, 1999).

12. Christopher Bollas, *The Shadow of the Object: Psychoanalysis of the Unthought Known* (New York: Columbia University Press, 1987).

13. Ibid., 285.

14. See D. W. Winnicott, *Holding and Interpretation: Fragment of an Analysis* (London: Hogarth Press, 1986).

15. See Cathy Caruth, "Interview with Jean Laplanche" (2001), at http://www.iath.virginia.edu/pmc/text-only/issue.101/11.2caruth.txt, para. 92l, for a way of understanding that might situate this ejaculatory suicide in relation to masochism: "I'm very critical about the term 'death drive,' and . . . I have called it a sexual death drive, with the emphasis more on 'sexual' than on 'death.' For me, the sexual death drive is just sexuality, unbound sexuality, the extreme of sexuality. And more than death, I would point to primary masochism. I see more of a sense of the sexual death drive in masochism or in sado-masochism than in death. And it was not on the side of sadism, but on the side of masochism, that Freud placed the core of his death drive."

16. Franz Kafka, "Cares of a Family Man" in *The Complete Stories*, trans. Willa and Edwin Muir (New York: Schocken, 1976), 427–28; "Die Sorge des Hausvaters," in *Die Erzählungen* (Frankfurt am Main: S. Fischer, 1998), 343–44.

17. It would be interesting to consider the two forms of "living on" in terms of the distinction between *fortleben* and *überleben* that Benjamin develops in "The Task of the Translator" (*Illuminations*, ed. Hannah Arendt, trans. Harry Zohn [New York: Schocken, 1968], 69–82). Clearly, both the final voice in "The Judgment" and the perpetuity of Odradek evoke the sense of *nachleben*, or living on. Significantly, Jacques Derrida references this difference between an afterlife (*überleben*) and a kind of survival or living

on (*fortleben*) that takes place in language to the presumption of human finitude. This operation of language is at once ghostly and animated. See his final interview, *Le Monde*, August 18, 2004.

18. Theodor W. Adorno, *Prisms*, trans. Samuel and Shierry Weber (Cambridge: MIT Press, 1981), 253; "Prismen" in Adorno, *Kulturkritik und Gesellschaft I, Gesammelte Schriften* (Frankfurt am Main: Suhrkamp, 1997): 10.1:9–287, here 264–65.

19. See John Fletcher, "The Letter in the Unconscious: The Enigmatic Signifier in Jean Laplanche," in *Jean Laplanche: Seduction, Translation, and the Drives*, ed. John Fletcher and Martin Stanton (London: ICA, 1992). Fletcher makes clear that Laplanche's recourse to the "adult world" as the source of sexual messages is a significant departure from psychoanalytic accounts that assume that an Oedipal scene with Mother and Father structures desire at a primary level. Fletcher recapitulates Laplanche's debt to and departure from the work of Jacques Lacan along these lines. At the end of his essay, Fletcher notes that Laplanche's theory of the "enigmatic signifier" emerges as a clear alternative to the Lacanian symbolic.

This counters the paternal law, linked to the structuralist account of the exchange of women and the universalist premises of "culture," with a conception of the enigmatic signifier, which assumes not only that primary unconscious and sexual messages are impressed upon the child (constituting the meaning and efficacy of "primary seduction") but that the primary others who make those impressions are themselves in the grip of similar messages, which can never be fully decoded or recovered. Indeed, as Fletcher puts it, "The Oedipus is no longer primal in the sense of the first, but topographically located as secondary, even though it may involve the re-elaboration of earlier inscriptions and translations, and it is no longer primal in the sense of universal but culturally contingent" (118).

Fletcher closes his essay on two notes. First, he asserts that Laplanche has clearly inaugurated a psychoanalytic possibility for explaining "those psychic trajectories that swerve from or attempt to rework the normalizing function of the paternal Law and its Oedipal polarities (e.g., various female and male homosexualities)." Although Fletcher does not show us precisely how this might work, he holds out this possibility as following from the displacement of the paternal law by the enigmatic signifier. Second, he points to a future project, namely, how to account for gender in the wake of the Oedipus's displacement from primacy: "What Laplanche's reworking of the drives in the context of primary seduction now leaves unclear or untheorised, is how the psychic constitution and inscription of a sexually and genitally differentiated body image (the repression and symbolization of what enigmatic signifiers?), the ground or at least terrain for the formation of gendered identities, is now to be rethought" (119).

20. Jean Laplanche, "The Drive and the Object-Source: Its Fate in the Transference," in *Jean Laplanche: Seduction, Translation, and the Drives*, ed. Fletcher and Stanton, p. 191; "La Pulsion et son objet-source: Son destin dans le transfert," in Laplanche, *Le Primat de l'autre en psychanalyse* (Paris: Flammarion, 1997), 227–242. As a textual source for this position, see Sigmund Freud, "The Unconscious," *The Standard Edition of the Complete Psychological Works of Sigmund Freud*, ed. James Strachey (London: Hogarth, 1953–74), 14:201–4, for the distinction between a word- and a thing-presentation in the unconscious.

21. Cathy Caruth, "Interview with Jean Laplanche" (2001), para. 124.

22. Laplanche, "The Drive and the Object-Source," 193.

23. Cathy Caruth, "Interview with Jean Laplanche" (2001), para. 89.

24. Jean Laplanche, "Responsabilité et réponse," *Entre séduction et inspiration: L'Homme* (Paris: Presses Universitaires de France, 1999), 147–72. All English translations in the text are mine.

CHAPTER 3. RESPONSIBILITY

1. Thomas Keenan conducts a lucid and provocative reading of both Levinas and Blanchot on the responsibility that arises from the situation of being held hostage. In the course of his exposition, he explains that the self who would respond to the address of the other is precisely not a personal self, but an "anyone," thus situating responsibility as a prerogative of anonymity. See Thomas Keenan, *Fables of Responsibility: Aberrations and Predicaments in Ethics and Politics* (Stanford: Stanford University Press, 1997), 19–23.

2. See the 1968 version of "Substitution" in Emmanuel Levinas, *Basic Philosophical Writings*, ed. Adriaan T. Peperzak, Simon Critchley, and Robert Bernasconi (Bloomington: Indiana University Press, 1996), 93–94; hereafter

cited in the text as S. This essay was subsequently reworked in *Otherwise than Being*.

3. Emmanuel Levinas, *Difficult Freedom: Essays on Judaism*, trans. Sean Hand (Baltimore: The Johns Hopkins University Press, 1990), 89; *Difficile Liberté: Essais sur le judaïsme* (Paris: Albin Michel, 1976). Hereafter cited in the text as *DF*. I consider this text at greater length in an unpublished essay, "Prehistories of Postzionism: The Paradoxes of Jewish Universalism."

4. Jean Laplanche, *Life and Death in Psychoanalysis*, trans. Jeffrey Mehlman (Baltimore: The Johns Hopkins University Press, 1985).

5. Theodor Adorno, *Minima Moralia: Reflections from Damaged Life*, trans. E. F. N. Jephcott (London: Verso, 1974), 164; *Minima Moralia: Reflexionen aus dem beschädigten Leben* (Frankfurt am Main: Suhrkamp, 1969), 216.

6. For an extended comparison of Adorno and Levinas, see Hent de Vries, *Minimal Theologies: Critiques of Secular Reason in Adorno and Levinas*, trans. Geoffrey Hale (Baltimore: The Johns Hopkins University Press, 2005).

7. See also Adorno's discussion of Kafka's tale in Theodor W. Adorno and Walter Benjamin, *The Complete Correspondence, 1928–1940*, ed. Henri Lonitz, trans. Nicholas Walker (Cambridge: Harvard University Press, 1999), 68–70; *Adorno-Benjamin Briefwechsel, 1928–1940*, ed. Henri Lonitz (Frankfurt am Main: Suhrkamp, 1995), 93–96.

8. See Max Weber on two forms of ethics, an ethics of responsibility and one of conviction, in "Politics as a Vocation," in *From Max Weber: Essays in Sociology*, trans. and ed. H. H. Gerth and C. Wright Mills (New York: Oxford University Press, 1958), 77–128. He argues that "conduct can be oriented to an 'ethic of ultimate ends' or to an ethic of responsibility" (120). The ethic of ultimate ends relates to a conviction that a certain end justifies the means required to achieve it and sometimes risks engaging morally dubious means for that purpose. An ethic of responsibility is attuned to the consequences of human conduct in the existing world and agrees to take responsibility for them. The position of "responsibility" is thus conduct-oriented and realistic. Weber ends up arguing that something of the idealism of the "ethic of ultimate ends" is required for a political vocation and that "an ethic of ultimate ends and an ethic of responsibility are not absolute contrasts but rather supplements, which only in unison constitute a genuine man—a man who can *have* a 'calling for poli-

tics'"(127). See also Wendy Brown, *Politics Out of History* (Princeton: Princeton University Press, 2001), 91–95.

9. Michel Foucault, "How Much Does It Cost for Reason to Tell the Truth?" in *Foucault Live*, ed. Sylvère Lotringer, trans. John Honston (New York: *Semiotext[e]*, 1989). The interview was first published as "Structuralism, Poststructuralism" in *Telos* 16, no. 55 (1983): 195–211, and it seems to have appeared simultaneously in German as "Um Welchen Preis sagt die Vernunft die Wahrheit," with Gerard Raulet, trans. Khosrow Nosration, in *Spuren* 1 and 2 (May and June 1983). The original interview, conducted in French, can be found as "Structuralisme et poststructuralisme," in Foucault, *Dits et Ecrits, 1954–1988*, vol. 4 (Paris: Gallimard), 431–457. The citations in the text are to *Foucault Live* in English as well as to *Dits et Ecrits*. The article in English is referred to as HM in the text; the interview in French is referred to as SP in the text. Translations of the latter are my own.

10. Michel Foucault, "About the Beginning of the Hermeneutics of the Self," trans. Thomas Keenan and Mark Blasius, *Political Theory* 21, no 2 (May, 1993): 198–227, republished in Michel Foucault, *Religion and Culture*, ed. Jeremy Carrette (New York: Routledge, 1999), 158–81. Citations in this text, from the latter volume, are referred to as H.

11. Foucault refers to a "form of power [that] imposes upon [the subject] a law of truth which he must recognize and which others have to recognize in him" in "The Subject and Power," in *Michel Foucault: Beyond Structuralism and Hermeneutics*, ed. Hubert Dreyfus and Paul Rabinow (Evanston, Ill.: Northwestern University Press, 1982), 212.

12. Ibid.

13. Ibid., 217.

14. *Parrhesia* is a Greek term for free-spokenness and frankness, linked to "license." It has two meanings. The first is "candid speech," and the second, "begging pardon in advance for necessary candor," according to Richard Lanham, *A Handbook of Rhetorical Terms* (Berkeley: University of California Press, 1991), 110. See Michel Foucault, *L'Herméneutique du sujet: Cours au Collège de France. 1981–82* (Paris: Gallimard, 2001), 355–78. Future citations to this volume are referred to as *HDS*; the translation into English is my own.

15. Michel Foucault, *Fearless Speech*, ed. Joseph Pearson (New York: Semiotext[e], 2001). This text is not written by Foucault but rather consists of

lectures derived from a transcription of one auditor's notes taken during a seminar called "Discourse and Truth" at Berkeley in the spring of 1983. Citations to this text are to *FS*. *L'Herméneutique du sujet: Cours au Collège de France. 1981–82* (see the previous note) includes similar preliminary material, especially on Seneca, asceticism, and *parrhesia*, but also extensive discussions of Alcibiades, Socrates, the delphic oracle, Epicurean and Stoic alternatives, the care of the self, and subjectivation.

INDEX